dd
26

Introduction to Antennas

Macmillan New Electronics Series
Series Editor: Paul A. Lynn

Paul A. Lynn, *Radar Systems*
A. F. Murray and H. M. Reekie, *Integrated Circuit Design*
Martin S. Smith, *Introduction to Antennas*

Introduction to Antennas

Martin S. Smith

MA, PhD, CEng, MIEE
Senior Principal Research Engineer, S.T.L., Harlow
formerly
Lecturer in Electronic Engineering, University College London

Macmillan New Electronics
Introductions to Advanced Topics

MACMILLAN
EDUCATION

First published 1988

Published by
MACMILLAN EDUCATION LTD
Houndmills, Basingstoke, Hampshire RG21 2XS
and London
Companies and representatives
throughout the world

Printed in Hong Kong

British Library Cataloguing in Publication Data
Smith, Martin S.
    Introduction to antennas.—(Macmillan
    new electronics).
    1. Antennas (Electronics)
    I. Title
    621.38′028′3   TK7871.6

ISBN 0–333–44558–9
ISBN 0–333–44559–7 Pbk

For my wife Sandy and
for my brother Steve

Contents

Contents

Series Editor's Foreword

The rapid development of electronics and its engineering applications ensures that new topics are always competing for a place in university and polytechnic courses. But it is often difficult for lecturers to find suitable books for recommendation to students, particularly when a topic is covered by a short lecture module, or as an 'option'.

Macmillan New Electronics offers introductions to advanced topics. The level is generally that of second and subsequent years of undergraduate courses in electronic and electrical engineering, computer science and physics. Some of the authors will paint with a broad brush; others will concentrate on a narrower topic, and cover it in greater detail. But in all cases the titles in the Series will provide a sound basis for further reading of the specialist literature, and an up-to-date appreciation of practical applications and likely trends.

The level, scope and approach of the Series should also appeal to practising engineers and scientists encountering an area of electronics for the first time, or needing a rapid and authoritative update.

Preface

Antennas are a vital part of many communication and radar systems, as they form and control the link between cable and radiative transmission of signals. As such they are usually an important topic in final year undergraduate courses and M.Sc. courses in Electronic Engineering and related disciplines. This book is intended to cover the theory and practice of antennas at a level suitable for such courses; it should also be a useful introduction to the subject for recently qualified engineers working in industry.

The first five (of six) chapters treat the basic theoretical analysis and experimental techniques. The main topics are wire antennas, aperture antennas, linear arrays and antenna measurements. There is an extensive literature covering more advanced and specialised antenna topics. The final chapter of this book includes a small selection of these topics, mainly associated with phased arrays. These have been chosen on the grounds that they contain some important principles of which a future antenna, or system, designer should be aware. Each chapter contains a case study of a practical application to illustrate the work of the chapter.

Thanks are due to many colleagues who have passed on their own experience to me. I am particularly indebted to the following people.

Dr Kenneth Budden supervised my research in radio wave propagation. Mr Norman Pavey first introduced me to antennas, particularly for aircraft use. Professor 'Den' Davies led me into various microwave antenna research topics, while Professor Alec Cullen introduced me to lecturing on antennas. I would also like to thank Mrs Margaret Ringsell for her expert typing of the manuscript.

Martin S. Smith

List of Symbols

c	speed of light *in vacuo*
d	array element spacing
d	antenna linear dimension
dB	decibel, $10 \log_{10}$ (power ratio)
f	frequency
$g_a(S_1, S_2)$	active element gain pattern
h	height
$h(S_1, S_2)$	array factor for a planar array
$\hat{u}$	unit vector
x, y, z	Cartesian coordinates
ρ, θ, z	cylindrical polar coordinates
r, θ, ϕ	spherical polar coordinates
$\boldsymbol{A}$	magnetic vector potential
A	geometrical area
A_e	effective area
A_{el}	area per element in a planar array
$\boldsymbol{B}$	magnetic flux intensity
C	$\cos \theta$
C, C'	contours of integration
$\boldsymbol{D}$	electric flux intensity
D	directivity
$\boldsymbol{E}$	electric field
$G(\theta, \phi)$	gain function
G	gain
$\boldsymbol{H}$	magnetic field
I	current
$I(\phi)$	circular array excitation
$\boldsymbol{J}$	current density
$J_m(x)$	Bessel function of order m
$\boldsymbol{M}$	magnetic current density
P, P_T, P_R	power, transmitted power, received power
$P(S), P(S_1, S_2)$	angular spectrum in two dimensions, three dimensions
R	measurement range length
R	circular array radius
R_{in}	real part of input impedance
R_{rad}	radiation resistance

R_{ohmic}	ohmic loss resistance
S	power flux density
S	$\sin \theta$
S_1, S_2	$\sin \theta \cos \phi$, $\sin \theta \sin \phi$
dS	element of surface area
X_{in}	imaginary part of input impedance
Z_{in}	input impedance
Z_0	characteristic impedance of free space, 377Ω
Z_0	transmission line characteristic impedance
ϵ_0	permittivity of free space
ϵ_r	relative permittivity (dielectric constant)
η	efficiency
θ	polar coordinate
λ	wavelength
μ_0	permeability of free space
μ_r	relative permeability
μ_{eff}	effective μ_r
σ	conductivity
σ	radar cross-section
τ	tilt angle of polarisation ellipse
ϕ	spherical polar coordinate
ϕ_n	circular array element angular coordinate
ϕ	incremental phase shift
ψ	any field component
ω	angular frequency
Γ	reflection coefficient

1 Basic Antenna Concepts

1.1 Introduction

Antennas are basic components of any electronic system which depends on free space as a propagation medium. An antenna is a device which provides a means for radiating or receiving radio waves. It is a transducer between a guided electromagnetic wave and an electromagnetic wave propagating in free space. In a communications link, the transmitter is connected through a cable or waveguide to one antenna, the signal is radiated to another antenna, and then passes through another cable or waveguide to the receiver.

Why not use a cable all the way? The answer is clearly dependent on the system requirements and what is convenient — for example, a modern telephone system uses optical fibres over shorter distances, but may use microwave radiated links over longer distances. Communications between aircraft and airfields must use free space propagation, as do radar and navigation systems. Broadcast systems such as TV or radio can use one transmitter to serve many receivers via a free space link.

1.2 From ELF to mm waves

Figure 1.1 shows the band designations for the commonly used radio frequency ranges. The wavelengths (λ) involved vary enormously; for example, at 100 Hz in the ELF band, $\lambda = 3000$ km, whereas at 100 GHz $\lambda = 3$ mm. Antenna dimensions can vary from very small fractions of a wavelength to many wavelengths. This suggests, correctly, that antennas take very different forms for different frequency bands. Some examples of antennas over the full range of frequencies are now briefly described.

Figure 1.2(a) shows an ELF 'electrode pair' antenna (Burrows, 1978) which, despite a length of 300 metres, is only 0.1 per cent of the free space wavelength at 100 Hz. Submarines can receive ELF signals using this antenna towed behind them as part of a cable, while still submerged. Higher frequency signals are too rapidly attenuated by sea water for underwater radio communications.

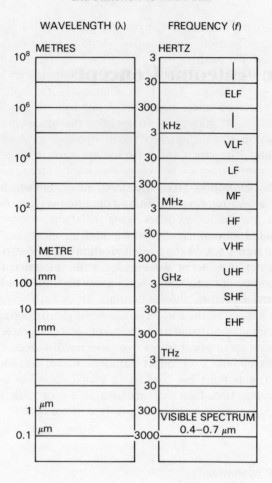

Figure 1.1 Frequency band designations

Figure 1.2(b) shows an HF (3–30 MHz) notch antenna on an aircraft. A portion of metal at the base of the tailfin is replaced by fibre glass so that a loop antenna can be formed, fed across the 'notch' with the return path through the fuselage. In fact, the notch antenna also induces r.f. currents in the whole airframe, so that the aircraft becomes part of the antenna. This is because the aircraft length is comparable with the wavelength (30 metres at 10 MHz).

Figure 1.2(c) shows the familiar UHF TV antenna, a 'Yagi' type. Only one element (cross piece) is fed from the cable, and currents induced in the other elements channel the radiation into (or out of) a narrow beam pointing along the row of elements. This both increases signal strength and reduces interference from reflected signals. 'Ghosts' on a TV screen are created by such reflections, which arrive later and hence are displaced on the time-scanned TV picture.

Figure 1.2(d) shows a paraboloid reflector antenna, with a waveguide 'horn' source at its focus. The horn illuminates the reflector, which collimates the radiation into a pencil beam just as a car headlight does at optical frequencies. At microwave frequencies the beam spreads out as a result of diffraction, and the antenna 'beam' becomes a cone of angles. As we shall see later, the larger the reflector aperture in wavelengths, the narrower that cone of angles becomes. Reflector antennas are used for microwave communication links, including via satellite, and in radar systems. They are by far the simplest and cheapest way of obtaining very narrow beams and the consequent 'gain' in signal strength, provided accurate direction pointing can be maintained.

Figure 1.2(e) shows a microstrip patch antenna array. Both the transmission line and the antenna array elements are made as printed circuits. Such antennas have some limitations, but are particularly useful in situations where a conformal (that is, flush mounted) structure is wanted.

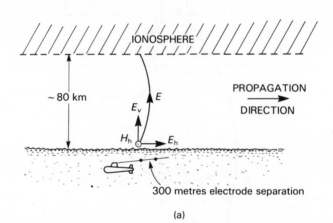

(a)

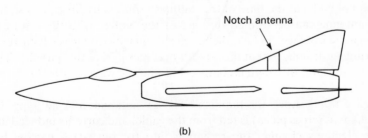

(b)

Figure 1.2 (continued overleaf)

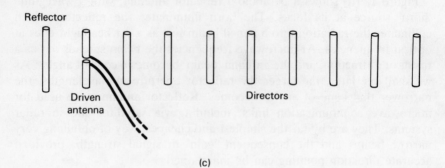

(c)

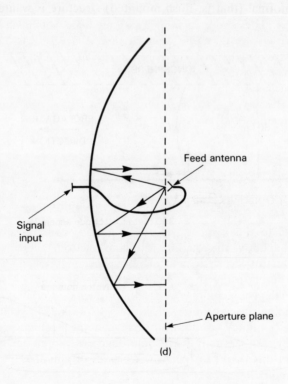

(d)

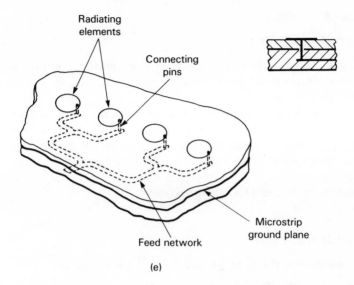

(e)

Figure 1.2 (a) ELF 'electrode pair' antenna (reproduced, with permission, from Burrows, M. L., *ELF Communications Antennas*, Peter Peregrinus, 1978). (b) HF notch antenna on an aircraft. (c) UHF TV 'Yagi' antenna. (d) Parabolic reflector antenna. (e) Microstrip patch antenna array (reproduced, with permission, from James, J. R., Hall, P. S. and Wood, C., *Microstrip Antenna Theory and Design*, Peter Peregrinus, 1981)

1.3 Maxwell's equations and plane waves

Antennas radiate and/or receive electromagnetic waves. Maxwell's equations allow us to derive the relations for plane electromagnetic waves. Both Maxwell's equations as such, and plane waves as particular solutions of them, will be used in the subsequent sections and chapters. All electromagnetic problems, including radiation problems, can in principle be solved by finding the appropriate solution of Maxwell's equations which fits the given boundary conditions. Some general techniques for solving antenna problems — usually with some degree of approximation — will be outlined in this book, for particular classes of antenna.

Maxwell's equations are

$$\text{div } \boldsymbol{D} = \rho \tag{1.1}$$

$$\text{div } \boldsymbol{B} = 0 \tag{1.2}$$

$$\text{curl } \boldsymbol{E} = -\partial \boldsymbol{B}/\partial t \tag{1.3}$$

$$\text{curl } \boldsymbol{H} = \boldsymbol{J} + \partial \boldsymbol{D}/\partial t \tag{1.4}$$

(Here $\boldsymbol{J}$ is current density and ρ is charge density.) Expressions for the vector differential operators div, grad, curl and ∇^2 are given in appendix A.

We shall consider a particular value of frequency, and assume a time factor $\exp(j\omega t)$, where $f = \omega/2\pi$ is the frequency in Hertz. This time factor will be suppressed throughout; to find the instantaneous value of any field variable, the $\exp(j\omega t)$ factor must be brought back explicitly before taking the real part.

Equations (1.3) and (1.4) then become

$$\text{curl } \boldsymbol{E} = -j\omega \boldsymbol{B} \tag{1.5}$$

$$\text{curl } \boldsymbol{H} = \boldsymbol{J} + j\omega \boldsymbol{D} \tag{1.6}$$

The constitutive relations for linear, isotropic media are

$$\boldsymbol{B} = \mu_r \mu_0 \, \boldsymbol{H}, \quad \boldsymbol{D} = \epsilon_r \epsilon_0 \, \boldsymbol{E}, \quad \boldsymbol{J} = \sigma \boldsymbol{E} \tag{1.7}$$

where $\mu_0 = 4\pi \times 10^{-7}$ H/m, $\epsilon_0 \approx \dfrac{1}{36\pi} \times 10^{-9}$ F/m

(Here μ_r is relative permeability, ϵ_r is relative permittivity and σ is conductivity.)

In free space:

$$\mu_r = \epsilon_r = 1, \quad \sigma = 0 \tag{1.8}$$

Two important quantities are

$$c = \frac{1}{\sqrt{(\mu_0 \, \epsilon_0)}} \approx 3 \times 10^8 \text{ m/s, the velocity of light } \textit{in vacuo}$$

$$Z_0 = \sqrt{\left(\frac{\mu_0}{\epsilon_0}\right)} \approx 377\Omega, \text{ the impedance of free space}$$

Using (1.8), equations (1.5) and (1.6) become

$$\text{curl } \boldsymbol{E} = -j\omega \, \mu_0 \, \boldsymbol{H} \tag{1.9}$$

$$\text{curl } \boldsymbol{H} = +j\omega \, \epsilon_0 \, \boldsymbol{E} \tag{1.10}$$

Expressing (1.9) and (1.10) in Cartesian coordinates:

$$\frac{\partial E_y}{\partial x} - \frac{\partial E_x}{\partial y} = -j\omega \, \mu_0 \, H_z$$

$$\frac{\partial E_z}{\partial y} - \frac{\partial E_y}{\partial z} = -j\omega \, \mu_0 \, H_x \tag{1.11}$$

$$\frac{\partial E_x}{\partial z} - \frac{\partial E_z}{\partial x} = -j\omega\,\mu_0\,H_y$$

$$\frac{\partial H_y}{\partial x} - \frac{\partial H_x}{\partial y} = j\omega\,\epsilon_0\,E_z$$

$$\frac{\partial H_z}{\partial y} - \frac{\partial H_y}{\partial z} = j\omega\,\epsilon_0\,E_x \tag{1.12}$$

$$\frac{\partial H_x}{\partial z} - \frac{\partial H_z}{\partial x} = j\omega\,\epsilon_0\,E_y$$

For a single plane wave, we can choose the z-axis to be its direction of propagation. We look for a solution of (1.11) and (1.12) with E and H having no variation with x or y (hence 'plane'). If we put $\partial/\partial x = \partial/\partial y = 0$, we find

$$E_z = H_z = 0 \tag{1.13}$$

$$\frac{-\partial E_x}{\partial z} = j\omega\,\mu_0\,H_y \tag{1.14}$$

$$\frac{-\partial H_y}{\partial z} = j\omega\,\epsilon_0\,E_x \tag{1.15}$$

$$\frac{\partial E_y}{\partial z} = j\omega\,\mu_0\,H_x \tag{1.16}$$

$$\frac{\partial H_x}{\partial z} = j\omega\,\epsilon_0\,E_y \tag{1.17}$$

(1.14) and (1.15) only include E_x and H_y, whereas (1.16) and (1.17) only include E_y and H_x. These pairs of equations describe the two independent linear polarisations. Eliminating H_y between (1.14) and (1.15), we obtain

$$\frac{\partial^2 E_x}{\partial z^2} + k^2\,E_x = 0 \tag{1.18}$$

where $k = \omega\sqrt{(\mu_0\,\epsilon_0)} = \omega/c = 2\pi/\lambda$ \tag{1.19}

The solution of the wave equation (1.18) is

$$\left.\begin{aligned} E_x &= A\,\exp(-jkz) + B\,\exp(+jkz) \\ H_y &= \frac{1}{Z_0}\,(A\,\exp(-jkz) - B\,\exp(+jkz)) \end{aligned}\right\} \tag{1.20}$$

The $\exp(-jkz)$ solution is a plane wave travelling in the positive z direction, while the $\exp(+jkz)$ solution is a plane wave travelling in the negative z direction. Note that $|E_x/H_y| = Z_0$ for each wave separately. The time-averaged Poynting vector, S, describing the power flux density in the wave, can be found from the complex forms of E and H, as

$$S = Re\{\tfrac{1}{2} E \times H^*\} = \frac{A^2}{2Z_0} \cdot u_z \text{ for the } \exp(-jkz) \text{ solution}$$

$$\frac{-B^2}{2Z_0} \cdot u_z \qquad\qquad \text{for the } \exp(+jkz) \text{ solution}$$

(where u_z is a unit vector in the $+z$ direction).

The basic results derived here will be used in chapters 2 and 3 for wire antennas and aperture antennas respectively.

1.4 Basic antenna properties

Despite the considerable differences in physical realisation of antennas for different frequencies and purposes, there are certain basic common properties which can be defined. The properties most often of interest are the *radiation pattern*, *gain*, *polarisation* and *impedance*. For a linear passive antenna, these properties are identical for either transmitting or receiving by virtue of the *reciprocity theorem*.

The *radiation pattern* of an antenna determines the spatial distribution of the radiated energy. For example, a vertical wire antenna gives uniform coverage in the horizontal (azimuth) plane, with some vertical directionality, and can therefore be used for broadcasting. For many directional antennas the important properties of the radiation pattern are the beam-width and the level of sidelobes (subsidiary maxima) in planes passing through the beam maximum. Figure 1.3 shows a typical directional radiation pattern. The *beamwidth* in a particular plane is usually defined by the angular width of the pattern at a level which is 3 dB down from the beam maximum. The *sidelobe level* is specified with reference to the maximum of the main beam and is generally expressed in dB down from it.

The directional characteristics of an antenna are frequently expressed in terms of a gain function $G(\theta, \phi)$, whose maximum value is the *gain*. (Here θ and ϕ are spherical polar angular coordinates.) This is now discussed for the transmit case, for convenience. The gain is defined as the ratio of the maximum radiation intensity from the antenna to the maximum from a reference antenna with the same input power. The reference is usually a hypothetical lossless isotropic radiator, and the gain can then be expressed in dBi. (It is worth noting that there is no such thing as a completely isotropic antenna.) At a distance r from an isotropic source, the power transmitted is evenly spread over a spherical surface of area $4\pi r^2$.

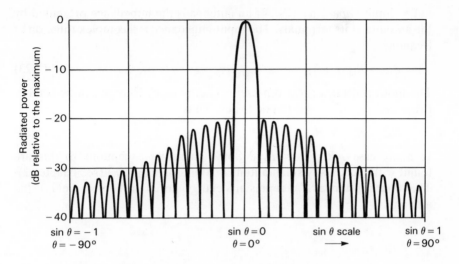

Figure 1.3 Directional radiation pattern

For an antenna with gain, it follows that the power P incident on an area A at a distance r in the direction of most intense radiation is

$$P = G \cdot P_T \cdot A/(4\pi r^2) \qquad (1.21)$$

where P_T is the transmitter power, and G is now used for the gain, the maximum value of $G(\theta, \phi)$. *Directivity*, D, is defined as the ratio of the maximum radiation intensity to the average radiation intensity (averaged over all angles). For an antenna which is 100 per cent efficient and has no copper, dielectric or mismatch loss, directivity and gain are the same. For an antenna with losses, G will be less than D by a factor corresponding to the efficiency, η:

$$G = \eta \cdot D \qquad (1.22)$$

The *polarisation* of an antenna is usually defined in terms of the orientation of the radiated electric field E in the direction of maximum radiation. For example, a vertical wire antenna is vertically polarised (see chapter 2). Circular (continuously rotating) polarisation can also be used, produced by two perpendicular linearly polarised fields with a 90° phase difference ($\pm90°$ giving left or right hand circular polarisation). Co-polarised radiation denotes energy radiated with the wanted polarisation, for example vertically polarised, or right hand circularly polarised. Cross-polarised radiation is energy radiated with the unwanted polarisation; in the above two cases, this would be horizontal, or left hand circular, polarisation.

The input *impedance*, Z_{in}, of an antenna is the impedance presented by the antenna at its terminals. The input impedance is a complex function of frequency:

$$Z_{in} = R_{in} + j\,X_{in} \tag{1.23}$$

The input resistance, R_{in}, represents energy used. Energy can be used in two ways, radiation and ohmic losses. Thus

$$R_{in} = R_{rad} + R_{ohmic} \tag{1.24}$$

In many cases, $R_{ohmic} \ll R_{rad}$. Some particular exceptions to this are found with electrically small antennas (dimensions $\ll \lambda$) (see chapter 2). The input reactance, X_{in}, represents energy stored in the near field of the antenna.

1.5 Reciprocity and receiving antennas

The reciprocity theorem for linear, passive, bilateral circuits tells us that we can interchange the positions in the circuit of a voltage (or current) source and an ammeter (or voltmeter) without altering the ammeter (or voltmeter) reading. A similar relation applies to antennas if the propagation medium and the antennas are linear, passive and isotropic. Thus if a transmitter is connected to antenna A, and a receiver to antenna B, the signal strength received is unchanged if the transmitter and receiver are interchanged. We can now use the reciprocity theorem to show that the transmit and receive radiation patterns of an antenna are identical.

Figure 1.4 shows one antenna, A, radiating, with a second antenna, B, receiving at a position (r_0, θ, ϕ). If we now move B to other positions (r_0, θ', ϕ'), while maintaining its orientation and polarisation relative to the radius from A, the variation of the received signal strength defines the radiation pattern of antenna A when transmitting. If the transmitter and receiver are now interchanged, the signal strength received by antenna A has an identical variation with θ and ϕ. Thus the receive pattern (the sensitivity variation) for antenna A is identical to its transmit pattern. An important consequence of this is that the gain of an antenna is identical for transmit and receive.

It will be shown in chapter 3 that the gain of a radiating aperture containing a uniform electric field over an area A is

$$G_a = \frac{4\pi A}{\lambda^2} \tag{1.25}$$

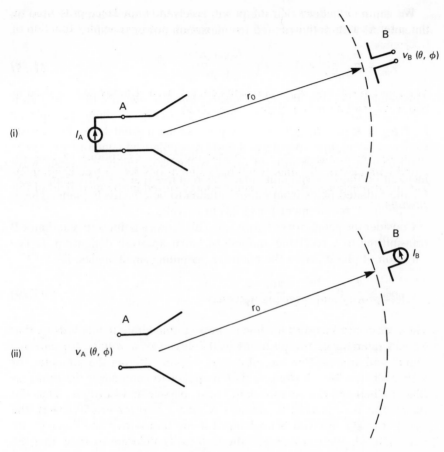

Figure 1.4 Antenna pattern reciprocity

Any antenna, of whatever form, has a value of gain, G. We can use (1.25) to define the *effective area* A_e of an antenna as

$$A_e = \frac{\lambda^2 G}{4\pi} \tag{1.26}$$

If we illuminate the uniform aperture antenna with a plane electromagnetic wave (of matching polarisation) with power density S (watts m^{-2}), the power received is $S \cdot A$. An antenna with different gain G will receive G/G_a times as much power (as a result of the reciprocity theorem). It therefore receives a power P_R:

$$P_R = S \cdot A_e \tag{1.27}$$

A_e is therefore the effective collecting area of the antenna on receive.

We can now deduce that the power received by an antenna B from an antenna A, with both oriented for maximum power transfer, is

$$P_R = \frac{G_A \cdot P_T}{4\pi r^2} \cdot A_e = P_T \cdot \frac{G_A G_B \lambda^2}{(4\pi r)^2} \qquad (1.28)$$

This relation is called the *Friis transmission formula*. If either antenna is not aligned for maximum power transfer, G_A or G_B can simply be replaced by the gain function $G(\theta, \phi)$. Any polarisation mismatch can be allowed for by resolving into co-polarised and cross-polarised components.

Implicit in the derivation of (1.28) is the assumption of a plane wave incident on the receiving antenna. This requires that r is sufficiently large for the radiated fields from either antenna to be effectively plane. This is the 'far field' requirement for (1.28) to be valid.

Consider the geometry of figure 1.5. This shows a point source radiator P transmitting to a receiving antenna of linear aperture dimension d. The variation of phase across the aperture, assuming small angles, is

$$\delta\phi \approx \frac{d}{2} \cdot \theta \cdot \frac{2\pi}{\lambda} \approx \frac{\pi d}{\lambda} \cdot \frac{d}{2r} \qquad (1.29)$$

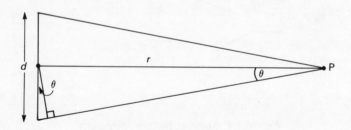

Figure 1.5 The Rayleigh criterion

The *Rayleigh criterion* for the transition between near and far field regions allows a phase variation across the received wavefront of 45°, or $\pm 22\frac{1}{2}°$. This occurs when

$$r = 2d^2/\lambda \qquad (1.30)$$

and this value of r is called the *Rayleigh distance*. If both antennas are of significant extent, with maximum aperture dimensions of d_1 and d_2, the far field criterion becomes

$$r > 2 (d_1^2 + d_2^2)/\lambda \qquad (1.31)$$

1.6 Choice of frequency

Radio wave propagation characteristics are important in the choice of frequency for a given communication or radar system. At ELF and VLF the waves travel around the earth as if they were in a waveguide bounded by the earth's surface and the ionosphere. Waves at LF and MF propagate either as surface waves guided by the curvature of the earth or as sky waves, reflected from the ionosphere. Sky waves allow communication over longer distances, but they are subject to fading — variations of signal strength due to ionospheric fluctuations. HF propagation is also by sky wave. Different frequencies have to be used at different times depending on propagation conditions. Short-range HF links can use ground waves, which are a combination of surface waves and waves reflected by the ground.

At VHF and UHF propagation is by a combination of direct and ground reflected waves ('space waves'), over relatively short distances (tens or hundreds of km). SHF and EHF propagation is also by space waves, and is consequently limited to line-of-sight links. At millimetric wavelengths, atmospheric attenuation becomes significant — though this can be used to advantage in covert communications.

Other factors of major importance are as follows. The radiation pattern required depends on the type of system, either broadcast or point to point (communication links or radar). Highly directional patterns require antenna dimensions of many wavelengths, with obvious consequences at low frequencies. The bandwidth required is dependent on the amount and type of information transmitted; FM radio uses greater bandwidth than AM to obtain superior quality of reproduction. Clearly the bandwidth available increases with increasing frequency — which is why FM radio uses carrier frequencies of the order of 100 MHz and AM radio of the order of 1 MHz. Limitations of very high frequencies are losses, difficulty in generating high power, and the complexity, cost and availability of suitable components.

Ambient noise is an important factor for frequencies around 1 MHz or lower. Atmospheric noise is then usually much greater than receiver noise, so that a receiving system is 'external noise limited'. Relatively low efficiency in a receive antenna for these frequencies — such as in a transistor radio — can consequently be tolerated. Under these conditions, the signal-to-noise ratio is independent of the antenna efficiency, unless it is so inefficient that the thermal noise becomes comparable to the received external noise.

The above criteria can be illustrated by considering typical uses of the various frequencies. ELF and VLF radio waves have worldwide range and are used to send signals to ships and submarines. VLF phase measurements are used for navigation. At ELF, the skin depth in sea water is relatively large, so submarines can receive signals while submerged. These are receive only systems as a mobile transmit antenna would be $\ll \lambda$ and hence inefficient (see chapter 2). The information rate is low, because of the small bandwidth used.

At LF and MF, mobile or household antenna efficiency is low, so a radio broadcast system with a single large transmit antenna and high power transmitter, and many receive only antennas, is appropriate. For a reasonable number of channels, about 10 kHz bandwidth can be used. AM is then the appropriate modulation system.

At HF, λ = 100–10 m, so antennas whose lengths are reasonable fractions of a wavelength are more readily available. Reasonable transmit efficiency is then possible, allowing two-way communication links. The bandwidth available (f = 3–30 MHz) allows many speech channels, and reflection by the ionosphere affords long ranges.

VHF and UHF offer two-way communications over tens or hundreds of kilometres. Sufficient bandwidth is available for FM radio broadcasting ($f \sim 100$ MHz) or TV broadcasting ($f \sim 600$ MHz in the UK), which requires 8 MHz channel spacing. Two-way communication links also use VHF and UHF.

The transmit antennas for AM radio, FM radio and TV are typically vertical masts, for uniform coverage in azimuth (for vertical polarisation), and some directivity in the elevation plane. (For horizontal polarisation, an array of horizontal polarised elements stacked vertically can be used.)

Receive antennas for these three cases are very different from one another. For AM radio, reception is external noise limited, so an inefficient, low gain, antenna can be used. A coil on a ferrite rod is a simple and small antenna which can be fitted into a domestic radio. This is a form of loop antenna (see chapter 2) and has a radiation pattern with a null ($\equiv$ zero or minimum) along its axis (for a radio wave arriving from that direction there is no component of magnetic field parallel to the rod). A simple rotation of the radio (and hence antenna) avoids the null.

For FM radio, an adequate signal-to-noise ratio demands a reasonably efficient receive antenna. A half-wave dipole (two $\lambda/4$ arms fed with a twin or coaxial transmission line, see chapter 2) offers of the order of unity gain in most directions (it again has a null along its axis). The polarisation (electric field) of the transmitted signal should ideally match the dipole orientation — a number of transmit stations now use 'mixed' polarisation to accommodate various receive antenna orientations. In addition, propagation effects at these frequencies can affect the polarisation received.

At TV frequencies, the receive antenna needs reasonable gain to give sufficient power transfer (see equation (1.28)). A Yagi antenna (figure 1.2, also chapter 2) has a fair amount of gain (an 18 element Yagi has ~15 dB gain) with a limited bandwidth. It is a cheap way of obtaining gain, and the bandwidth can be made adequate for a reasonably closely spaced set of TV channels. However, in areas served by different transmitters, Yagis designed for different bands are needed. Their fairly narrow beamwidths (20–30°) mean that reasonably accurate pointing is required.

At frequencies greater than 1 GHz, large bandwidths and hence high information rates are available. However, the Friis transmission formula, equation (1.28), shows that the power received is proportional to λ^2 if the antenna gains are fixed. Hence received power falls rapidly with increasing frequency. The power that can be generated readily also falls off as the frequency increases. High gain antennas must therefore be used, so that point-to-point, rather than broadcast, systems are generally used. These include microwave links, radar systems and communications via satellite. A geostationary satellite orbits at about six earth radii, so that even a high gain antenna illuminates a substantial fraction of the earth's surface. Direct broadcast by satellite (DBS) is therefore feasible. DBS reception requires a high gain antenna pointing to the appropriate satellite.

Limitations at very high frequencies arise with very high gain antennas, as these require high accuracy of antenna shape and their very narrow beamwidth requires accurately maintained pointing. Propagation effects which vary the angle of arrival can now be significant, as well as atmospheric attenuation at millimetric wavelengths.

1.7 Antenna analysis and design

So far we have considered antenna properties which are common to any antenna type. In order to undertake detailed analysis of antennas, some quite distinct techniques are required for different classes of antenna. Wire antennas (chapter 2), such as dipoles or Yagis, are analysed through the radiating properties of r.f. (radio frequency) *currents*. Aperture antennas (chapter 3), such as horns and reflectors, are analysed using the radiating properties of *fields*. Antenna arrays (chapter 4) are sampled apertures, and their analysis is equivalent to a discrete series, rather than an integral, form of aperture theory.

Exact theories for antennas are not usually available, and the experimental measurement of antenna properties (chapter 5) is a vital part of antenna development and design.

Analysing a particular antenna configuration is one side of a coin. The design of antennas requires the other side — synthesis. Particular antenna properties are specified — for example, radiation pattern, bandwidth, etc. We then have an 'inverse' problem — and for antennas, as with most physical situations, this is more difficult than the analysis problem. In certain cases systematic synthesis procedures are available, such as for linear arrays or shaped reflectors. Even then, realisability can be a problem — for example, if a synthesised array excitation has too rapid a phase variation, the array tolerances become critical and the system bandwidth becomes limited. The approximations inherent in the analysis may be invalidated by the mathematical results, for example, if a deduced reflector profile varies significantly within a wavelength.

Phased arrays are a very important class of antenna, as their excitations, and hence their radiation patterns, can be electronically controlled. Array radiation patterns can therefore both be synthesised, and varied — for example, a narrow beam can be scanned electronically to point in different directions, without the antenna (array) moving physically. Chapter 6 introduces some more advanced properties of antenna arrays than are covered in chapter 4.

Reference

Burrows, M. L. (1978). *ELF Communication Antennas*, Peter Peregrinus, Hitchin, Herts.

2 Wire Antennas

2.1 Introduction

As was briefly mentioned in section 1.7, 'wire' antennas are analysed through the radiating properties of r.f. currents on wires. The simplest wire antenna is the dipole, shown in figure 2.1(a). It is usually easier to derive the radiating properties of antennas when transmitting, and then to invoke the reciprocity theorem for receive. For the dipole of figure 2.1, an r.f. voltage is applied to the terminals, and r.f. currents are set up in the dipole arms. These currents radiate into free space, with a characteristic radiation pattern, gain and polarisaion.

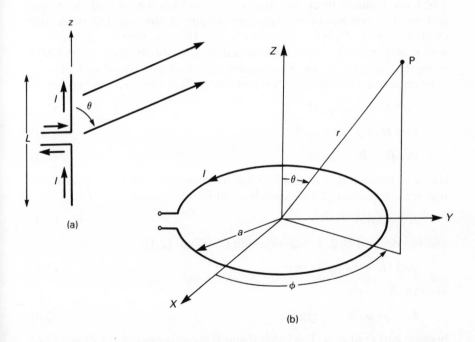

Figure 2.1 (a) Dipole antenna. (b) Loop antenna

17

The standard TV reception antenna is a more complex wire antenna, called a Yagi antenna (section 2.4), and this is shown in figure 1.2(c). The Yagi consists of a dipole antenna, plus additional wire elements which serve to reshape the radiation pattern to give more gain than a simple dipole.

Another simple wire antenna is the loop antenna shown in figure 2.1(b). This is a 'dual' of a dipole, with electric and magnetic fields interchanged (section 2.5). A multi-turn loop with a ferrite core is often used as a receiving antenna in AM radios.

The aircraft notch antenna of figure 1.2(b) is a loop, although currents induced in the main aircraft fuselage also act as a dipole in combination. The calculation of the currents induced in complex structures can be made using 'moment methods' (section 2.7).

2.2 The Hertzian dipole

The basic building block for wire antenna calculations is derived in this section. This consists of an expression for the electromagnetic fields of a current element, $I \, \delta l$ ($I = I_0 \exp(j\omega t)$), the 'Hertzian dipole'. The fields of a wire antenna with known or assumed current distribution can be found using this basic result, by summing contributions from small sections.

From section 1.3, Maxwell's equations for free space can be written as

$$\text{curl } E = -j\omega \, \mu_0 \, H \tag{2.1}$$

$$\text{curl } H = J + j\omega \, \epsilon_0 \, E \tag{2.2}$$

$$\text{div } H = 0 \tag{2.3}$$

(div $D = \rho$ is not used explicitly in the following derivation.) Note that J is non-zero. Equation (2.3) is used to establish the identity

$$H = \text{curl } A \tag{2.4}$$

because div curl $\equiv 0$. If we substitute (2.4) into (2.1):

$$\text{curl } (E + j\omega \, \mu_0 \, A) = 0 \tag{2.5}$$

We can then write:

$$E + j\omega \, \mu_0 \, A = -\text{grad } \phi \tag{2.6}$$

because curl grad $\equiv 0$. The fields E and H are expressed by (2.4) and (2.6) as functions of potential functions ϕ and A (the electrostatic potential and the magnetic vector potential respectively). We now need to find ϕ and A for particular problems.

Substituting (2.4) into (2.2):

$$\text{curl curl } A = j\omega\,\epsilon_0\,E + J \tag{2.7}$$

A standard vector identity converts the left hand side of (2.7) into

$$\text{grad div } A - \nabla^2 A$$

Substituting (2.6) into (2.7) then gives

$$\text{grad div } A - \nabla^2 A = j\omega\,\epsilon_0\,(-j\omega\,\mu_0\,A - \text{grad }\phi) + J$$

which can be recast as

$$\nabla^2 A + \omega^2\,\mu\epsilon_0\,A - \text{grad}(j\omega\epsilon\,\phi + \text{div }A) = -J \tag{2.8}$$

We are, in fact, free to specify div A, and a convenient mathematical choice is the 'Lorentz condition':

$$\text{div } A = -j\omega\epsilon\phi \tag{2.9}$$

Then (2.8) simplifies to

$$\nabla^2 A + \omega^2\,\mu_0\,\epsilon_0\,A = -J \tag{2.10}$$

Once (2.10) has been solved to find A for a specified current density J, ϕ can be obtained from (2.9) and then E and H found.

For rectangular Cartesian coordinates, (2.10) can be separated into x, y and z components, for example

$$\nabla^2 A_z + k^2\,A_z = -J_z \tag{2.11}$$

where $k^2 = \omega^2\,\mu_0\,\epsilon_0$. Now consider an infinitesimal z-directed current element placed at the origin, so that only $A_z \neq 0$. For all points except at the origin

$$\nabla^2 A_z + k^2\,A_z = 0 \tag{2.12}$$

Writing ∇^2 in spherical polar coordinates (r, θ, ϕ), and using spherical symmetry, the solutions to (2.12) are $C\exp(-jkr)/r$ and $D\exp(+jkr)/r$. The physically meaningful solution (outgoing waves) is the first of these. The multiplying constant for a unit impulse function source is $1/4\pi$, so for the current element considered

$$A_z = \frac{\exp(-jkr)}{4\pi r}\cdot I\,\delta l \tag{2.13}$$

The electric and magnetic fields can be found from (2.13), and the mathematical details are given in appendix B. The results are:

$$H_\phi = \frac{I\,\delta l}{4\pi} \cdot jk \left(1 + \frac{1}{jkr}\right) \frac{\exp(-jkr)}{r} \sin\theta$$

$$E_\theta = \frac{I\,\delta l}{4\pi} \cdot jk\, Z_0 \left[1 + \frac{1}{jkr} + \frac{1}{(jkr)^2}\right] \frac{\exp(-jkr)}{r} \sin\theta \qquad (2.14)$$

$$E_r = \frac{I\,\delta l}{2\pi} \cdot jk\, Z_0 \left[\frac{1}{jkr} + \frac{1}{(jkr)^2}\right] \frac{\exp(-jkr)}{r} \cos\theta$$

If kr is large, that is, if $r \gg \lambda$, all terms including inverse powers of jkr are very small, and in the 'far field', $E_r = 0$, and

$$H_\theta = \frac{I\,\delta l}{4\pi} \cdot jk \frac{\exp(-jkr)}{r} \sin\theta$$

$$E_\theta = \frac{I\,\delta l}{4\pi} \cdot jk\, Z_0 \frac{\exp(-jkr)}{r} \sin\theta \qquad (2.15)$$

Thus E and H are at right angles and in the ratio $E/H = Z_0$, just as for the plane waves of section 1.3. The factor $\sin\theta$ is the radiation pattern of the Hertzian dipole. The $1/r^2$ and $1/r^3$ terms in (2.14) are only significant in the reactive 'near field', $r < \lambda$.

The average power radiated by an antenna is

$$P_{\text{rad}} = \tfrac{1}{2} R_{\text{rad}} |I_{\text{in}}|^2 \qquad (2.16)$$

where R_{rad} is the radiation resistance and I_{in} is the current at the input terminals. The radiated power for a Hertzian dipole $I\,\delta l$ can be found from

$$P_{\text{rad}} = \tfrac{1}{2} \iint E \times H^* \cdot dS \qquad (2.17)$$

Here $dS = r^2 \sin\theta \, d\theta \, d\phi$ and using (2.15), this leads to

$$P_{\text{rad}} = \frac{k^2 Z_0}{12\pi} \cdot (I\,\delta l)^2 \qquad (2.18)$$

The radiation resistance is then

$$R_{\text{rad}} = \frac{2P_{\text{rad}}}{I^2} = \frac{k^2 Z_0}{6\pi} (\delta l)^2$$

$$= \left(\frac{2\pi}{\lambda}\right)^2 \cdot \frac{120\pi}{6\pi} \cdot (\delta l)^2 = 80\pi^2 \left(\frac{\delta l}{\lambda}\right)^2 \qquad (2.19)$$

If $\delta l \ll \lambda$, R_{rad} is very small. The radiation efficiency is

$$\eta = R_{\text{rad}}/(R_{\text{rad}} + R_{\text{ohmic}}) \qquad (2.20)$$

Ohmic resistance is proportional to the dipole length, whereas R_{rad} is proportional to (length)^2. Then for 'electrically small' antennas (length $\ll \lambda$), the radiation efficiency is in general poor. This is a basic limitation of electrically small antennas.

Another factor which limits the performance of such antennas is their large input reactance, X_{in} (equation (1.23)). A short dipole has a capacitive reactance, and an electrically small loop antenna has an inductive reactance. The short antenna has thus a very high 'Q'. For reasonable power transfer, a matching network is needed to 'tune out' the antenna reactance, and this can lead to further losses, or a narrow bandwidth. The 'efficiency –bandwidth product' is strictly limited for electrically small antennas.

2.3 Dipoles and monopoles

The current distribution on a Hertzian dipole is uniform — however, the current on a straight wire antenna must in fact go smoothly to zero at the ends. The current distribution on a short centre-fed wire dipole of length δl ($\ll \lambda$) is approximately triangular in shape. The effective length of such an antenna is half of its physical length, and its radiation resistance is

$$R_{rad} = 20\pi^2 \left(\frac{\delta l}{\lambda}\right)^2 \tag{2.21}$$

Compared with the Hertzian dipole, the input current is similar, but the average current is halved. The radiated power (compare equation 2.18) is reduced by a factor of 4, and so is the radiation resistance.

For thin wire antennas (diameter $\ll$ length) the current distribution is approximately sinusoidal, with zeros at the wire ends. Thus, for a *half-wave dipole*, with total length $= \lambda/2$, the current distribution is (see figure 2.2(a))

$$I(z) = I_m \cos kz, \quad |z| \leq \lambda/4 \tag{2.22}$$

Equation (2.15) gives the radiated fields for a current element $I\,\delta l$. The radiation pattern of the half-wave dipole is calculated by superposing contributions from elements δl, allowing for their relative positions.

Figure 2.1(a) shows the geometry. Equation (2.15) contains a factor $\exp(-jkr)/r$, and in the far field

$$r(z) = r_0 - z \cos \theta \tag{2.23}$$

where r_0 is the distance from the centre of the dipole.

The important effect is the relative phase variation, so the radiated field

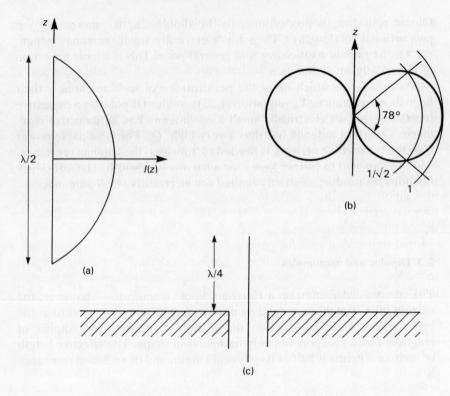

Figure 2.2 (a) Half-wave dipole. (b) Radiation pattern. (c) Quarter-wave
    monopole

for a half-wave dipole antenna is

$$E_\theta = \frac{jk\,Z_0}{4\pi} \cdot I_{\mathrm m} \sin\theta \cdot \frac{\exp(-jkr)}{r} \int_{-\lambda/4}^{+\lambda/4} \cos kz \cdot \exp(jkz\cos\theta)\,\mathrm{d}z$$

$$= \frac{j\,Z_0}{2\pi} \cdot I_{\mathrm m} \frac{\exp(-jkr)}{r} \cdot \frac{\cos(\pi/2\cos\theta)}{\sin\theta} \qquad (2.24)$$

The radiation pattern of a half-wave dipole is thus

$$\cos(\pi/2\cos\theta)/\sin\theta \qquad (2.25)$$

and this is shown in figure 2.2(b) in polar coordinate form. It is not in fact
very different from the pattern of a short dipole ($\sin\theta$); the 3 dB
beamwidth is 78° rather than 90°.

The importance of the half-wave dipole is that the input reactance is zero
for a length very close to $\lambda/2$ (a few per cent less for typical wire

thicknesses). The input resistance for this length is $\approx 70\Omega$. Coaxial cables with characteristic impedances of 50Ω or 75Ω are usually used to feed antennas, so a half-wave dipole is a well-matched load.

A *monopole* antenna is so called because it is effectively half a dipole. A standard case is a $\lambda/4$ length of wire which is fed from a coaxial cable through a metal ground plane, as in figure 2.2(c). The electrical image of the monopole forms the other half of a dipole (for an ideal infinite ground plane). Consequently, the radiation pattern of a $\lambda/4$ monopole is the same as that of a $\lambda/2$ dipole, above the ground plane. As it radiates nothing below the ground plane, the gain of an ideal monopole is 3 dB higher than for a dipole (5.2 dBi rather than 2.2 dBi). The input impedance is half that of a dipole twice the length; for example, a monopole just less than $\lambda/4$ long has an input impedance $\approx 35\Omega$. A 50Ω cable is a fair match to either a dipole (70Ω) or a monopole.

Input impedance data for monopoles (and hence dipoles) with various lengths and wire thicknesses are given in Jasik (1961). For a cylindrical $\lambda/4$ monopole or $\lambda/2$ dipole of diameter d, the input bandwidth generally increases as d increases.

An important practical aspect of feeding dipole antennas is the use of a *balun* (short for 'balanced to unbalanced transformer'). A coaxial transmission line is not balanced, unlike a parallel wire line. Coaxial lines are normally used to minimise transmission loss. In a balanced mode, the currents on the inner conductor are equal and opposite to those on the inside of the outer conductor. If currents are induced, by the antenna, on the outside of the coaxial cable, the dipole currents become asymmetrical (the inner goes to one half of the dipole, the outer to the other half). The coax outer then becomes part of the radiating antenna, producing cross-polarisation. The use of a balun (either bought as a separate package, or built into the antenna design) suppresses the unbalanced mode described above (Jasik (1961) gives various balun designs.)

2.4 Parasitic elements

A Yagi (strictly Yagi–Uda) antenna (shown in figure 1.2(c)) is a good example of the use of parasitic elements. Figure 2.3(a) shows a three-element Yagi antenna, which demonstrates the basic Yagi design (Yagi, 1928). One element, typically a $\lambda/2$ dipole, is fed using a coaxial cable. This 'driven' element ('driver') excites currents in the other, parasitic, elements by near field coupling. If we know the currents (amplitude and phase distributions) on all the elements, we can superpose their radiated fields, allowing for relative position, to find the overall radiation pattern. The calculation of induced currents is complicated; the 'method of moments' (section 2.7 below gives a brief introduction) is a general technique applicable to structures up to a few wavelengths in size.

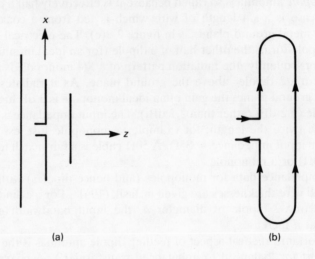

(a)   (b)

Figure 2.3 (a) Three-element Yagi antenna. (b) Folded dipole

Yagi and Uda found that the currents induced in a parasite which is slightly longer (~ 5 per cent) than the driver are such that the combined pattern has a maximum to the other side of the driver; consequently such a parasite is termed a 'reflector'. If the parasite is slightly shorter (~ 5 per cent) than the driver, the combined pattern has a maximum to the same side as the parasite, which is now termed a 'director'. Typical spacings between the elements are ~ 0.2λ. A three-element Yagi can give a gain of 9 dB. The addition of further directors increases the gain, although the improvements decrease rapidly with increasing number of elements. (Additional reflectors have little effect.)

The input impedance of a Yagi antenna is generally lower than that of an isolated dipole. A folded dipole driver is often used to increase the input impedance so as to give a better match to the 75Ω coaxial cable usually employed. A half-wave folded dipole antenna, shown in figure 2.3(b), has an input impedance about four times that of a λ/2 dipole.

An important limitation of Yagi antennas is their relatively narrow bandwidth — which is why a different Yagi is needed for TV reception in different areas. The main advantage of a Yagi antenna is that only one element needs to be fed, and this keeps the cost low.

2.5 Loops and slots

A small loop, figure 2.4(a), is the *dual* of a short dipole (small and short meaning $\ll \lambda$). Duality can be explained using Maxwell's equations. For an electric current source J_1, the fields E_1 and H_1 satisfy

$$\text{curl } E_1 = -j\omega \, \mu_0 \, H_1$$
$$\text{curl } H_1 = j\omega \, \epsilon_0 \, E_1 + J_1 \tag{2.26}$$

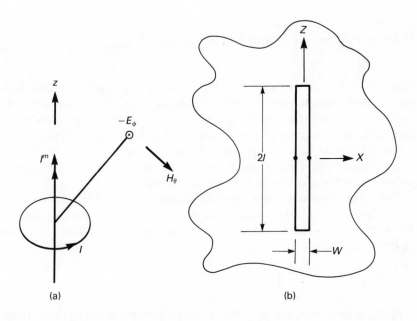

Figure 2.4 (a) Small loop antenna. (b) Rectangular slot antenna

A fictitious magnetic current source M_2 can be introduced into Maxwell's equations, to replace a complicated set of electric currents, and in that case:

$$\text{curl } E_2 = -j\omega \, \mu_0 \, H_2 - M_2$$
$$\text{curl } H_2 = j\omega \, \epsilon_0 \, E_2 \tag{2.27}$$

The equations (2.26) and (2.27) are equivalent if

$$E_2 \rightarrow -H_1, \quad H_2 \rightarrow E_1, \quad \mu_0 \longleftrightarrow \epsilon_0 \tag{2.28}$$

A small current loop can be represented as a fictitious magnetic dipole $I_m \, \delta l$, directed normal to the loop. The fields of an electric dipole element $I \, \delta l$ are given by (2.14) at any range, and by (2.15) in the far field.

The far fields of the loop can be found from (2.15) by applying the duality transformations (2.28), whence

$$E_\phi = \frac{-I_m \, \delta l}{4\pi} \cdot jk \, \frac{\exp(-jkr)}{r} \sin \theta$$

$$H_\theta = \frac{I_m \, \delta l}{4\pi} \cdot \frac{jk}{Z_0} \frac{\exp(-jkr)}{r} \sin \theta$$

(2.29)

If the loop carries a current I and has an area A:

$$I_m \, \delta l = jk \, Z_0 \, IA \tag{2.30}$$

This can be derived by calculating the far fields of a small loop (any shape can be used, though a square gives the simplest algebra), by summing the far fields of the electric current elements making up the loop (allowing for their different positions and orientations) and comparing with (2.29).

The amplitude radiation pattern of a small loop is just $\sin \theta$, as for a short dipole. The pattern nulls are normal to the loop. The antenna polarisations for a loop and a dipole are orthogonal.

The input impedance of a small loop antenna is very different from a short dipole. Its reactive component is inductive rather than capacitive. The radiation resistance can be found using equations (2.16), (2.17) and (2.29):

$$R_{rad} = 320\pi^4 \left(\frac{A}{\lambda^2} \right)^2 \tag{2.31}$$

Multiple turns increase R_{rad}; the magnetic moment is proportional to the number of turns n. The radiation resistance therefore increases as n^2. A ferrite core similarly increases the magnetic moment by a factor μ_{eff}, so

$$R_{rad} = 320\pi^4 \left(n \, \mu_{eff} \frac{A}{\lambda^2} \right)^2 \tag{2.32}$$

A multi-turn ferrite core loop antenna is commonly used for AM radio reception.

Figure 2.4(b) shows a rectangular slot cut in a large sheet of metal. A slot antenna can be fed by a transmission line connected across the narrow dimension of the slot, through a waveguide, or by exciting a cavity placed behind it. It may radiate to both sides of the sheet, or only on one side, depending on the feed configuration. Duality exists between a thin rectangular slot and a 'complementary' electric dipole which would just fill the slot (with the ground plane then removed). (Booker (1946) derives this duality.) Exchanging electric and magnetic quantities, as in (2.28), can therefore be used to give the fields of a short slot or a $\lambda/2$ slot from the corresponding fields for a short dipole or a $\lambda/2$ dipole.

The radiation pattern of a slot is therefore similar to that of a dipole with the slot orientation, but with an orthogonal polarisation. In figure 2.4(b), this means a uniform pattern in the x–y plane, and a zero along the z-axis. The electric field is E_ϕ relative to the z-axis — that is, in the x–y plane.

2.6 Printed antennas

Figure 2.5 shows a microstrip transmission line in cross-section. Such lines are often used in microwave circuits (Edwards, 1981). The characteristic impedance of the line is primarily determined by the ratio of the line width to the substrate thickness, and the relative permittivity ϵ_r of the substrate. Such lines can be made by selective etching of metal from one surface of metal-clad dielectric boards. Coaxial connections can be made either at board edges or through the board.

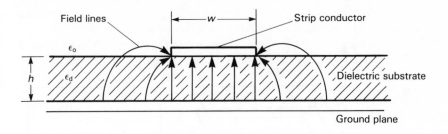

Figure 2.5 Microstrip transmission line

Figure 2.6 shows a printed dipole antenna, and the way it is interfaced directly to a printed feed line. One arm of the dipole is printed on each side of the dielectric board. This can be a very convenient way of constructing and feeding dipoles at frequencies above about 1 GHz.

Figure 2.7 shows a microstrip patch antenna, fed by (a) a microstrip transmission line, or (b) a coaxial connection through the board. Waves can propagate below the patch, but meet discontinuities at the patch edges. The patch therefore acts as a cavity, and has resonant modes. At the edges of the patch, there are fringing fields like those shown in figure 2.5. There is a region close to an edge where there is an electric field component in the plane of the patch. The radiation from an edge is similar to that from a slot antenna. With a feed as in figure 2.7(a), the two edges perpendicular to the feed line radiate and the resultant radiation pattern is found by

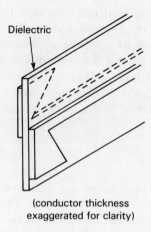

(conductor thickness
exaggerated for clarity)

Figure 2.6 Printed dipole antenna (reproduced, with permission, from James,
J. R., Hall, P. S. and Wood, C., *Microstrip Antenna Theory and
Design*, Peter Peregrinus, 1981)

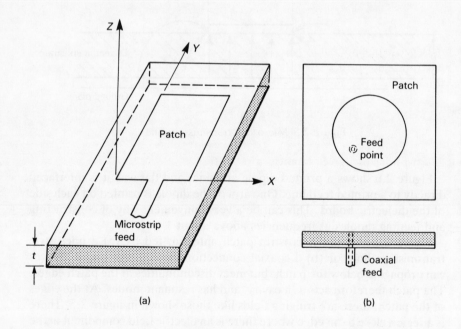

Figure 2.7 Microstrip patch antenna: (a) rectangular patch, microstrip feed;
(b) circular patch, coaxial feed

superposing the patterns of two slots separated by the patch length. A circular patch, figure 2.7(b), has a different set of resonant modes to a rectangular or square patch. The feed point is chosen for best impedance match. Figure 2.8 shows the radiation pattern of a circular patch excited in its lowest order mode.

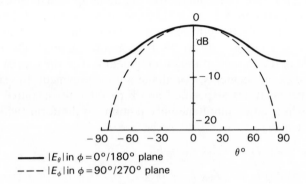

Figure 2.8 Radiation pattern of a circular patch antenna (reproduced, with permission, from James, J. R., Hall, P. S. and Wood, C., *Microstrip Antenna Theory and Design*, Peter Peregrinus, 1981)

Because patches act as resonant cavities, they generally have a relatively narrow bandwidth. Substrate thickness is an important parameter: the thinner the substrate, the narrower the bandwidth.

There are many forms for printed and microstrip antennas, and James *et al.* (1981) give a detailed exposition.

2.7 An introduction to moment methods

Earlier in this chapter, the calculation of the radiating properties of wire antennas was considered, given the r.f. current distribution on the wires. In simple cases, this can be assumed to be sinusoidal. In more complex situations, for example, a three-element Yagi antenna, the current distributions need to be derived. Moment methods (Moore and Pizer, 1984) are particularly useful for solving this sort of problem, usually with the aid of a computer. (The term 'method of moments' arises from the mathematics involved in solving the integral equations for the general case.)

The limits on how large an antenna structure can be treated can be seen by observing that it has to be divided into wire segments about $\lambda/10$ long, and the calculation involves the inversion of an $N \times N$ matrix, where N is the total number of segments.

The antenna problem is to deal with a specified source, such as the r.f. voltage applied to the terminals of the driven dipole in a Yagi antenna, and to satisfy the boundary condition that $E_{\text{tangential}} = 0$ at the surface of the wires. The unknown is the current $I(r)$; for electrically thin wires (diameter $\ll \lambda$), the currents can be assumed to be purely longitudinal.

In the simplest form of the method of moments applied to wire antennas, the wires are considered as made up of segments about $\lambda/10$ long, with a constant current I_n on the nth segment. (This implies current discontinuities where segments join, but works as an approximation.) The tangential electric field at the surface of the mth segment is then the sum of the fields produced by all the segments. For all but a source segment, this sum has to be zero, whereas it has a specified non-zero value for a source segment. This results in a set of simultaneous equations of the form (with a single source element)

$$Z_{11}\, I_1 + Z_{12}\, I_2 \ldots Z_{1N}\, I_N = E_0$$
$$Z_{21}\, I_1 + Z_{22}\, I_2 \ldots Z_{2N}\, I_N = 0$$

$$\ldots \ldots \ldots \ldots \ldots \ldots \ldots \ldots \ldots \ldots \tag{2.33}$$

$$Z_{N1}\, I_1 + Z_{N2}\, I_2 \ldots Z_{NN}\, I_N = 0$$

Here the boundary condition $E_{\text{tangential}} = 0$ has only been enforced at one point per segment (a further approximation), giving N equations for N unknowns. The coefficients Z_{ij} are a function of the relative position and orientation of the ith and jth segments. Expressions for them are given in Richmond (1966). Equation (2.33) can be expressed in matrix form and matrix inversion used to find the unknown currents I_n.

Once the current distribution is known, the radiation pattern can be found by superposing contributions from the N segments, allowing for their relative positions and orientations. The input impedance can be found as V_0/I_1, but in practice it is more difficult to make accurate predictions of input impedance than for radiation patterns. (Input impedance is a 'local' property which requires accurate modelling in the vicinity of the source.)

Antennas on metal structures such as aircraft or other vehicles can also be treated by the method of moments. The continuous metal surfaces are modelled by grids of wire segments, about $\lambda/10$ long; this approximate problem is then solved using the method of moments. This technique is usually called 'wire grid modelling', for obvious reasons. For three-dimensional structures like an aircraft, a maximum dimension of about 2λ can be accommodated, using several hundred segments. This limits the frequency range of application to HF (3–30 MHz) or lower, for aircraft (which are typically 15–20 metres long).

2.8 Case study: antennas on aircraft

An aircraft needs antennas for a variety of functions, principally communi-cation, navigation and radar. Communication frequencies vary from HF (from 2 MHz upwards) to VHF and UHF (up to 400 MHz). All-round radiation pattern coverage in the horizontal (azimuth) plane is required, over a reasonable range of elevation angles. Linear polarisation, usually vertical, is used. Satellite communication and navigation systems for aircraft generally operate at frequencies above 1 GHz. The antenna coverage required is typically over the upper hemisphere, with circular polarisation. Radar systems also tend to use frequencies above 1 GHz. A radar system usually requires a high gain antenna which can be steered to scan over a particular sector.

Aerodynamic and structural considerations place major constraints on the type and size of antennas which can be fitted. Figure 2.9 shows some typical aircraft antennas. The HF notch antenna has been described in section 1.2, and is clearly aerodynamically suitable. Structurally, however, the amount of metal which can be removed from the tail fin is limited, with the consequence that the notch 'loop' is rather small, and hence inefficient at the low HF frequencies. In order to cover a wide frequency band, an antenna tuning unit (ATU) with switched or variable capacitances and inductances is needed to match the input impedance to a 50Ω system.

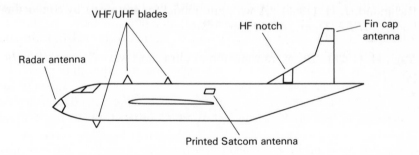

Figure 2.9 Antennas fitted to an aircraft

At VHF and UHF, 'blade' antennas are used, which are essentially monopoles made with a flat sheet rather than a cylinder. (A flat monopole of width 2*a* is electrically equivalent to a cylindrical monopole of diameter *a*.) The antenna is encased in a fibre glass shell which is shaped for minimum aerodynamic resistance. This shell also acts as the antenna's 'radome'. A radome is usually needed to protect an antenna from the weather or wind erosion, while still allowing the antenna to radiate. The top of the tail fin is often used to house antennas, by replacement of the metal tip section with a fibre glass shell containing flat sheet antennas.

Printed antennas are often used for satellite communication and navigation systems, because they can be mounted flush with the aircraft skin. An aircraft nose cone may be replaced by a fibre glass radome containing a small microwave reflector antenna (see chapter 3), which can be rotated vertically and horizontally for use as a forward-looking radar antenna.

References

Booker, H. G. (1946). 'Slot aerials and their relation to complementary wire aerials', *Journal IEE (London)*, pt. IIIA, *93*, pp. 620–6.

Edwards, T. C. (1981). *Foundations for Microstrip Circuit Design*, Wiley, New York.

James, J. R., Hall, P. S. and Wood, C. (1981). *Microstrip Antenna Theory and Design*, Peter Peregrinus, Hitchin, Herts.

Jasik, H. (Ed.) (1961). *Antenna Engineering Handbook*, McGraw-Hill, New York.

Moore, J. and Pizer, R. (Eds) (1984). *Moment Methods in Electromagnetics*, Research Studies Press, Letchworth, Herts.

Richmond, J. H. (1966). 'A wire grid model for scattering by conducting bodies'. *IEEE Trans.*, *AP-14*, pp. 782–6.

Yagi, H. (1928). 'Beam transmission of ultra short waves', *Proc. IRE*, *16*, pp. 715–41.

3 Aperture Theory

3.1 Diffraction by apertures

Figure 3.1(a) shows what happens to a plane electromagnetic wave incident on an aperture in an otherwise opaque screen, according to geometrical optics. The implication that the emerging beam has a sharp boundary, with fields suddenly falling to zero, violates Maxwell's equations. In fact, the beam edge is diffuse, and lateral spreading takes place. The rate of lateral spreading with distance can be found from a very simple argument, using figure 3.1(b). Consider the uniformly illuminated aperture of length a divided into two halves, with a point source at the centre of each half. At a certain angle, θ_0, the path difference to a distant point from the centres of the two halves is $\lambda/2$, so that the contributions made by them cancel and the field vanishes. The line BC represents the boundary between full field and zero field in the geometrical optics approximation. OA, the line at angle θ_0, intersects BC at a distance $z = z_0$ from the aperture. Then for $z \ll z_0$, geometrical optics is a good approximation. For $z \gg z_0$, 'Fraunhofer' diffraction theory applies. In this region, the beam spreads linearly with distance z; the first null in the diffraction pattern is given by (using the geometry of figure 3.1(b)):

$$\sin \theta_0 = \lambda/a \tag{3.1}$$

The distance z_0 can be evaluated using the relation

$$\tan \theta_0 = a/2z_0 \tag{3.2}$$

For small angles $\sin \theta_0 \approx \tan \theta_0$, whence

$$z_0 = a^2/2\lambda \tag{3.3}$$

This is of similar form to equation (1.30) for the Rayleigh distance — an exact correspondence of numerical factors is not expected, given the very simple model used. The dependence on a and λ is, however, fundamental.

In this chapter, the problem of finding the diffracted fields for a given 'aperture distribution' is solved using the technique of an angular spectrum of plane waves. An aperture distribution is a defined set of fields E and H in a source plane; in the example above, the source fields are assumed to have a uniform distribution over an aperture of width a. This example is essentially two dimensional, with no variation of fields out of the plane of

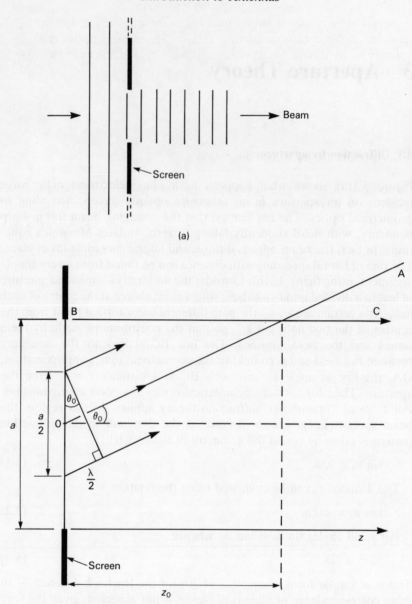

Figure 3.1 (a) Plane wave incident on an aperture. (b) Lateral spreading

the diagram. Aperture theory is developed firstly for two-dimensional problems, and then extended to the general three-dimensional case.

Antennas such as horns and reflectors are considered, for which the source fields can be defined over a plane aperture. Usually the aperture is assumed to be relatively large compared to the wavelength. If $a \gg \lambda$, the distance $z_0 \gg a$ (using equation (3.3)). Geometrical optics can consequently be used to define aperture distributions for reflector antennas, as in section 3.4 below.

3.2 Aperture theory in two dimensions

In section 1.3, Maxwell's equations were used to derive the equations of a plane wave travelling along the z-axis. The (transverse) electric field is

$$E = A \exp(-jkz) \tag{3.4}$$

for a wave travelling in the direction of z increasing. More generally:

$$E = A \exp(-jks) \tag{3.5}$$

where s represents distance measured along a straight line in the plane wave direction. Let s be as shown in figure 3.2, so that a plane wave is travelling at an angle α to the z-axis, in the x–z plane. The magnetic field H is parallel to the y-axis (for the particular linear polarisation shown). There is no y dependence of the fields, so we are considering a two-dimensional problem.

Then

$$E_x = E \cos \alpha$$
$$E_z = -E \sin \alpha \tag{3.6}$$
$$H_y = E/Z_0$$

and

$$\begin{aligned} s \;\; &= r \cos (\theta - \alpha) \\ &= r \cos \theta \cos \alpha + r \sin \theta \sin \alpha \\ &= z \cos \alpha + x \sin \alpha \end{aligned} \tag{3.7}$$

Combining (3.5), (3.6) and (3.7), the field components of the plane wave are

$$\begin{aligned} E_x &= A \cos \alpha \exp(-jk(z \cos \alpha + x \sin \alpha)) \\ E_z &= -A \sin \alpha \exp(-jk(z \cos \alpha + x \sin \alpha)) \\ H_y &= \frac{A}{Z_0} \cdot \exp(-jk(z \cos \alpha + x \sin \alpha)) \end{aligned} \tag{3.8}$$

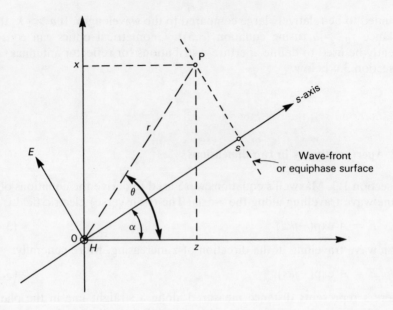

Figure 3.2 Plane wave at an angle

It can be readily shown that each of these three components satisfies the two-dimensional wave equation:

$$\frac{\partial^2 \psi}{\partial x^2} + \frac{\partial^2 \psi}{\partial z^2} + k^2 \psi = 0 \tag{3.9}$$

where

$\psi \equiv$ any of E_x, E_z, H_y. For example, let

$$\psi \equiv E_x: (-k^2 \sin^2 \alpha - k^2 \cos^2 \alpha + k^2)\psi = 0 \tag{3.10}$$

The power flux density in the wave, S, is found using the Poynting vector:

$$S = Re \left\{ \tfrac{1}{2} E \times H^* \right\} = \frac{A^2}{2Z_0} \cdot \{ u_z \cos \alpha + u_x \sin \alpha \} \tag{3.11}$$

where u_z and u_x are unit vectors along the axes; thus the power flow is indeed along s.

(The other independent linear polarisation has field components H_x, H_z and E_y, with expressions of the form (3.8).)

Equation (3.10) shows that (3.8) gives solutions of Maxwell's equations for any value of α, provided $\sin^2 \alpha + \cos^2 \alpha = 1$. This can in fact be satisfied for *complex* α. As an example of a complex α:

let

$$S = \sin \alpha > 1 \tag{3.12}$$

then

$$C = \cos \alpha = \pm j \cdot \sqrt{(S^2 - 1)}$$

The solution (3.8) then becomes

$$E_x = jA \sqrt{(S^2 - 1)} \cdot \exp(-jkxS) \cdot \exp(\pm kz \sqrt{(S^2 - 1)})$$

$$E_z = -A \cdot S \cdot \exp(-jkxS) \cdot \exp(\pm kz \sqrt{(S^2 - 1)}) \tag{3.13}$$

$$H_y = \frac{A}{Z_0} \exp(-jkxS) \cdot \exp(\pm kz \sqrt{(S^2 - 1)})$$

Now consider the components of the Poynting vector $Re\{\frac{1}{2} E \times H^*\}$. These are

$$Re\ \{\tfrac{1}{2} E_x H_y^*\}\ \boldsymbol{u}_z = Re\ \left\{ \frac{jA^2}{2Z_0} \sqrt{(S^2 - 1)} \cdot \exp(\pm 2kz \sqrt{(S^2 - 1)}) \right\} \boldsymbol{u}_z = 0$$

$$\tag{3.14}$$

$$Re\ \{-\tfrac{1}{2} E_z H_y^*\}\ \boldsymbol{u}_x = \frac{A^2}{2Z_0} \cdot S \cdot \exp(\pm 2kz \sqrt{(S^2 - 1)}) \cdot \boldsymbol{u}_x$$

This *inhomogeneous plane wave* has the following properties:

(i)   equal phase planes are $x = $ constant;
(ii) equal amplitude planes are $z = $ constant;
(iii) the power flux is along $\hat{x}$, perpendicular to the equiphase planes;
(iv) the wave is exponentially decaying away from $z = 0$.

The phase variation in the x direction corresponds to a wavelength less than the free space TEM value in the ratio $1/\sin \alpha$. The phase velocity is then $c/\sin \alpha < c$, so the wave is a 'slow wave' in the x direction. Such waves are also called 'surface' waves as they are confined to the vicinity of the plane $z = 0$. For real α, equation (3.8) describes a *homogeneous* plane wave, where the equal phase planes are also equal amplitude planes.

We are now in a position to introduce the concept of an 'angular spectrum of plane waves', which is used to derive aperture theory. This will allow us to deduce the radiation properties of aperture antennas, such as horns and parabolic reflectors.

For a simple plane wave:

$$E_x = E \cos \alpha$$

where $\tag{3.15}$

$$E = A \exp(-jk(z \cos \alpha + x \sin \alpha))$$

Since Maxwell's equations are linear, two plane waves in the x–z plane can be superposed. Then

$$E_x = E(\alpha_1) \cos \alpha_1 + E(\alpha_2) \cos \alpha_2 \tag{3.16}$$

More generally:

$$E_x = \sum_{n=1}^{\infty} E(\alpha_n) \cos \alpha_n \tag{3.17}$$

is also a permissible solution of Maxwell's equations.

Still more generally, we can write

$$E_x = \int E(\alpha) \cos \alpha \, d\alpha \tag{3.18}$$

where $E(\alpha)$ may now be a continuous function of α. Writing this in full:

$$E_x = \int A(\alpha) \cdot \cos \alpha \cdot \exp(-jk(z \cos \alpha + x \sin \alpha)) \, d\alpha \tag{3.19}$$

Changing the variable to $S = \sin \alpha$:

$$E_x = \int P(S) \exp(-jk(zC + xS)) \, dS \tag{3.20}$$

where

$$C = \sqrt{(1 - S^2)}, \quad P(S) = A(\alpha)$$

The function $P(S)$ is the 'angular spectrum'.

The limits of the integrals in (3.19) and (3.20) have not yet been defined. If we confine our attention to waves travelling out into the right hand half plane, $z > 0$, in figure 3.2, the obvious choice seems to be

$$-\pi/2 \leqslant \alpha \leqslant \pi/2$$

or

$$-1 \leqslant S(= \sin \alpha) \leqslant +1$$

However, complex values of α can also satisfy our plane wave equations. To decide which of these values are to be included requires a consideration of boundary conditions as $r(= \sqrt{(x^2 + z^2)})$ tends to infinity. We have restricted our solution to $z > 0$, but x can be > 0 or < 0. Observing the plane wave expression

$$\exp(-jk(z \cos \alpha + x \sin \alpha))$$

in the integrand of (3.19), we must have $\sin \alpha$ purely real to avoid exponential growth in either the $+x$ or $-x$ directions. If

$$|\sin \alpha| > 1, \quad \cos \alpha = \pm j\sqrt{(S^2 - 1)}$$

and we must choose the negative imaginary root to obtain decay rather than growth in the $+z$ direction.

If we write

$$E_x = \int_{-\infty}^{+\infty} P(S) \exp(-jk(zC + xS)) \, dS \qquad (3.21)$$

then this contains all the possible plane waves which satisfy our boundary conditions as $r \to \infty$.

We now consider the limits for equation (3.19) — that is, how α varies as $S = \sin \alpha$ varies from $-\infty$ to $+\infty$. We know that when $S = 1$, $\alpha = \pi/2$. Let $\alpha = \pi/2 + j\beta$. Then

$$\sin \alpha = \sin \pi/2 \cos j\beta + \cos \pi/2 \sin j\beta = \cosh \beta \qquad (3.22)$$

so that $\sin \alpha \geqslant 1$ and is real:

$$\cos \alpha = \cos \pi/2 \cos j\beta - \sin \pi/2 \sin j\beta = -j \sinh \beta \qquad (3.23)$$

To obtain exponential decay for $z > 0$ we therefore require $\beta > 0$. Figure 3.3(a) shows the *contour* of integration for (complex) α. For $S < -1$, a similar argument to that above shows that $\alpha = -\pi/2 + j\beta$ with β now required to be < 0.

The angular spectrum $P(\sin \alpha)$ has a simple physical significance which can be shown most clearly by considering the integrals in α for both E_x and E_z:

$$E_x = \int_C P(\sin \alpha) \exp(-jkr \cos(\theta - \alpha)) \cos \alpha \, d\alpha \qquad (3.24)$$

$$E_z = -\int_C P(\sin \alpha) \exp(-jkr \cos(\theta - \alpha)) \sin \alpha \, d\alpha \qquad (3.25)$$

Here polar coordinates r, θ are used from figure 3.2. These equations have the form

$$\psi = \int_C F(\alpha) \exp(-jkr \cos(\theta - \alpha)) \, d\alpha$$

$$\text{where } F(\alpha) = \begin{cases} P(\sin \alpha) \cos \alpha & \text{from (3.24)} \\ -P(\sin \alpha) \sin \alpha & \text{from (3.25)} \end{cases} \qquad (3.26)$$

As $kr \to \infty$ — the far field — the integrand of (3.26) oscillates extremely rapidly and generally makes a negligible contribution to the integral. The

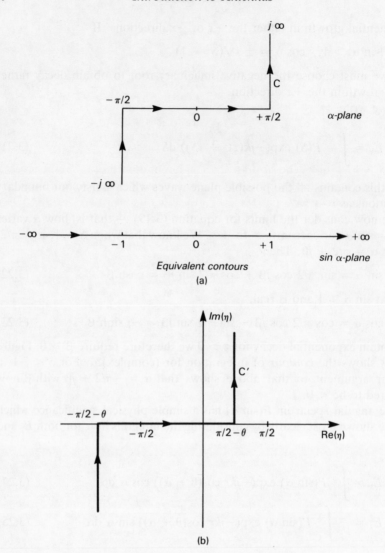

Figure 3.3 (a) Contour of integration C. (b) Contour C′

only significant contribution comes from values of α near $\alpha = \theta$, where the *phase is stationary* with respect to α, that is

$$\frac{\partial}{\partial \alpha}(kr \cos(\theta - \alpha)) = 0$$

Let

$$\alpha - \theta = \eta \qquad (3.27)$$

and write

$$\cos(\alpha - \theta) \approx 1 - \tfrac{1}{2}\eta^2 \tag{3.28}$$

$$d\alpha = d\eta \tag{3.29}$$

Then

$$\psi \approx \exp(-jkr) \int_{C'} F(\alpha) \exp\left(\frac{jkr}{2}\eta^2\right) d\eta \tag{3.30}$$

Figure 3.3(b) shows the contour C'. The major contribution to the integral comes from the vicinity of $\eta = 0$. In the limit as $kr \to \infty$, we can therefore discard the imaginary parts of C' and add the missing portions of the real η-axis. Both give negligible contributions to the integral when kr is very large. Then

$$\psi \approx \exp(-jkr) \int_{-\infty}^{\infty} F(\alpha) \cdot \exp\left(\frac{jkr}{2}\eta^2\right) d\eta, \tag{3.31}$$

$$\approx \exp(-jkr)F(\theta) \int_{-\infty}^{\infty} \exp\left(\frac{jkr}{2}\eta^2\right) d\eta \tag{3.32}$$

There is a standard integral:

$$\int_{-\infty}^{\infty} \exp(-ax)^2 \, dx = \sqrt{(\pi/a)} \tag{3.33}$$

This can be used when a is purely imaginary, as required here. Then

$$\psi \approx \exp(-jkr)\, F(\theta) \sqrt{\left(\frac{2\pi}{kr}\right)} \exp(j\pi/4) \tag{3.34}$$

If we now use (3.26), then when $kr \to \infty$:

$$E_x = P(\sin\theta)\cos\theta \sqrt{\left(\frac{2\pi}{kr}\right)} \exp(-j(kr - \pi/4))$$

$$E_z = -P(\sin\theta)\sin\theta \sqrt{\left(\frac{2\pi}{kr}\right)} \exp(-j(kr - \pi/4)) \tag{3.35}$$

$E_x = E\cos\theta$ and $E_z = -E\sin\theta$, and $E = \sqrt{(E_x^2 + E_z^2)}$. This is illustrated in figure 3.4, where E is demonstrated to be $E \cdot \hat{u}_\theta$. Thus

$$E_\theta = P(\sin\theta) \sqrt{\left(\frac{2\pi}{kr}\right)} \exp(-j(kr - \pi/4)) \tag{3.36}$$

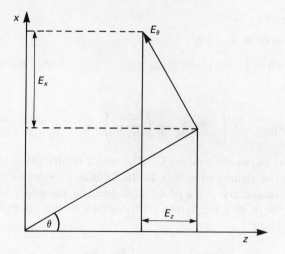

Figure 3.4 Far field components

Equation (3.36) makes the physical significance of the 'angular spectrum' $P(\sin \theta)$ clear; it corresponds to the radiation pattern at a great distance from the radiating aperture. Equation (3.36) is a product $f(\theta)$ $g(r)$. The dependence of E_θ on r can be explained as follows. We are considering a two-dimensional problem (no y dependence of fields), so we expect $E_\theta \propto 1/\sqrt{r}$ for conservation of energy in a cylindrical wave. The phase variation $\exp(-jkr)$ is also appropriate to a cylindrical wave ($r = \sqrt{(x^2 + z^2)}$). Even the $\pi/4$ phase shift can be explained as half the $\pi/2$ shift through a cylindrical focus — a known optical effect.

We next take up the question of how $P(\sin \theta)$ is to be calculated. Let us return to (3.21):

$$E_x(x, z) = \int_{-\infty}^{\infty} P(\sin \alpha) \exp(-jk(z \cos \alpha + x \sin \alpha)) \, d(\sin \alpha) \quad (3.37)$$

The field in the 'aperture' plane $z = 0$ is

$$E_x(x, 0) = \int_{-\infty}^{\infty} P(\sin \alpha) \exp(-jkx \sin \alpha) \, d(\sin \alpha) \quad (3.38)$$

This is a Fourier transform equation, like

$$f(t) = \int_{-\infty}^{\infty} F(\omega) \exp(j\omega t) \, d\omega \quad (3.39)$$

The inverse of (3.39) is

$$F(\omega) = \frac{1}{2\pi} \int_{-\infty}^{\infty} f(t) \exp(-j\omega t) \, d\omega \tag{3.40}$$

Equations (3.39) and (3.40) define the frequency spectrum $F(\omega)$ of a function of time $f(t)$. We can invert (3.38) in a similar manner, where $t \equiv kx$ and $\omega \equiv \sin \alpha$:

$$P(\sin \alpha) = \frac{1}{2\pi} \int_{-\infty}^{\infty} E_x(x, 0) \exp(+jkx \sin \alpha) \, d(kx)$$

$$= \frac{1}{\lambda} \int_{-\infty}^{\infty} E_x(x, 0) \exp(+jkx \sin \alpha) \, dx \tag{3.41}$$

(The difference between $+j$ in (3.39) and $-j$ in (3.38) is not significant; the important thing is to change sign for their respective inverses.) Thus the angular spectrum $P(\sin \alpha)$ can be calculated as the Fourier transform of the aperture distribution $E_x(x, 0)$. The Fourier transform relationship between a source distribution and its radiation pattern is the fundamental result of aperture theory. All the established properties of Fourier transforms may therefore be used.

Our solution (3.37) satisfied Maxwell's equations in the half space $z > 0$, and satisfied our boundary conditions as $r \to \infty$. We have now included the boundary conditions for the plane $z = 0$, and have thus obtained a defined solution. Equation (3.37) is valid for any $z > 0$, and shows that the electromagnetic field (here in two dimensions) can be represented by the addition of plane waves, including some inhomogeneous or 'surface' waves. Equation (3.36) is the much simpler form for (3.37) obtained in the far field ($kr \to \infty$). As was shown in its derivation, the surface waves make no contribution to the far field radiation pattern, and are associated with antenna near fields.

The above solution corresponds to one of the two possible independent linear polarisations; if $E_y(x, 0)$ is non-zero, a second angular spectrum exists. In principle, a knowledge of H_y or H_x in the plane $z = 0$ would also give the same electromagnetic solutions as E_x or E_y. In practice, E_x, say, is not known exactly, and is approximated in the solution of antenna problems. If simplifying assumptions such as $E_x/H_y = Z_0$ in the aperture are made, then the solution derived from H_y may not agree precisely with that derived from E_x. In some texts the quoted formula for radiation from apertures uses half of the E_x solution + half of the H_y solution! This will be made explicit for aperture theory in three dimensions, in section 3.4.

3.3 Applications of aperture theory

The basic result of aperture theory for two-dimensional problems is that the radiation pattern $P(\sin \alpha)$ is the Fourier transform of the aperture distribution $E_x(x, 0)$. Mathematically

$$P(\sin \alpha) = \frac{1}{\lambda} \int_{-\infty}^{\infty} E_x(x, 0) \cdot \exp(jkx \sin \alpha) \, dx$$

The calculation of radiation patterns for some standard aperture distributions will both illustrate the technique and derive several very important antenna properties. The first case is a uniform distribution, that is

$$E_x(x, 0) = \begin{cases} E_0, & -a/2 < x < a/2 \\ 0, & |x| > a/2 \end{cases} \tag{3.42}$$

Then the radiation pattern is

$$\begin{aligned} P(S = \sin \alpha) &= \frac{1}{\lambda} \int_{-a/2}^{+a/2} E_0 \cdot \exp(jkxS) dx \\ &= \frac{E_0}{\lambda} \left[\frac{\exp(jkxS)}{jkS} \right]_{-a/2}^{a/2} \\ &= E_0 \frac{a}{\lambda} \frac{\sin(kaS/2)}{kaS/2} \end{aligned} \tag{3.43}$$

Figure 3.5(a) shows $P(S)$. The radiation pattern peak is at $S = 0$, normal to the aperture, and the main beam extends from $S = -\lambda/a$ to $s = +\lambda/a$. The first sidelobe peak is at $S \approx \pm \frac{3}{2} \lambda/a$, and zeros of the pattern occur at $S = \pm n \, \lambda/a$. (Note the correspondence with equation (3.1), based on a simple diffraction model.) Negative values for $P(S)$ indicate a phase difference of 180° relative to the main beam.

Figure 3.5(b) shows the same pattern expressed on a dB scale, as $20 \log_{10}\{|P(S)|/|P|_{max}\}$. The first (and largest) sidelobe level is at -13.2 dB relative to the main beam peak. The two main features of a directive radiation pattern are the beamwidth (usually at the -3 dB level) and the sidelobe levels. Here the zero to zero beamwidth is $2\lambda/a$ on a $\sin \alpha$ scale, while the 3 dB beamwidth is $\approx 0.9 \, \lambda/a$.

The above case illustrates one very important antenna property, namely the inverse relationship between aperture size in wavelengths and the beamdwidth. Thus narrow beams require large apertures.

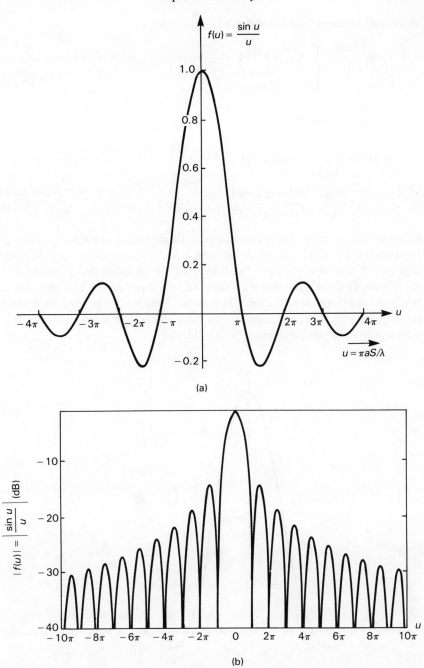

Figure 3.5 (a) Uniform aperture radiation pattern. (b) Radiation pattern in
          decibels

A second example is a half-cosine distribution:

$$E_x(x, 0) = \begin{cases} E_0 \cos\left(\dfrac{\pi x}{a}\right), & -a/2 \leqslant x \leqslant a/2 \\ 0, & |x| > a/2 \end{cases} \tag{3.44}$$

The radiation pattern is

$$P(S) = \frac{E_0}{\lambda} \int_{-a/2}^{a/2} \exp(jkxS) \frac{(\exp(j\pi x/a) + \exp(-j\pi x/a))}{2} \, \mathrm{d}x$$

$$= \frac{E_0 a}{\lambda} \cdot \frac{\pi/2 \cos(kaS/2)}{\pi^2/4 - k^2 a^2 S^2/4} \tag{3.45}$$

(after some algebra). This radiation pattern is plotted in figure 3.6 (linear field scale). The first zero of the pattern is *not* where $kaS/2 = \pi/2$, as both numerator and denominator become zero simultaneously. The zero-to-zero beamwidth is now $3\lambda/a$ on a $\sin \alpha$ scale, 50 per cent larger than for a uniform aperture distribution. The 3 dB beamwidth is also increased correspondingly. The sidelobe levels have decreased significantly — the first is now -23 dB (compared with -13 dB).

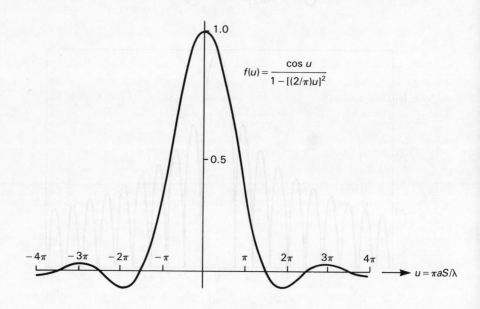

$$f(u) = \frac{\cos u}{1 - [(2/\pi)u]^2}$$

Figure 3.6 Half-cosine aperture radiation pattern

This second case illustrates another important antenna property; using a *tapered* aperture distribution (an 'amplitude taper') tends to reduce sidelobe levels (there are limits), at the expense of an increase in main beam width. Low sidelobes are often a very desirable property in various applications.

Table 3.1 lists four standard aperture distributions and the corresponding radiation patterns. The derivations for cases 3 and 4 are left as problems.

Table 3.1

Aperture distribution	Radiation pattern (normalised)	First sidelobe level
1. $f(x) = 1$ $\|x\| < a/2$	$P(S) = \dfrac{\sin(ka\,S/2)}{(ka\,S/2)}$	-13 dB
2. $f(x) = \cos(\pi x/a)$ $\|x\| < a/2$	$P(S) = \dfrac{\cos(ka\,S/2)}{1 - (ka\,S/\pi)^2}$	-23 dB
3. $f(x) = \cos^2(\pi x/a)$ $\|x\| < a/2$	$P(S) = \dfrac{\sin(ka\,S/2)}{(ka\,S/2)} \cdot \dfrac{1}{1 - (ka\,S/2\pi)^2}$	-32 dB
4. $f(x) = 1 - 2\|x\|/a$ $\|x\| < a/2$	$P(S) = \left\{ \dfrac{\sin(ka\,S/4)}{(ka\,S/4)} \right\}^2$	-26 dB

As a further example, consider a general amplitude distribution $A(x)$. The corresponding radiation pattern is

$$P(S) = \frac{1}{\lambda} \int_{-\infty}^{\infty} A(x)\, \exp(jkxS)\, dx$$

Now 'add' a linear phase variation across the aperture — that is, the aperture distribution becomes $A(x)\, \exp(j\beta x)$. Then the new radiation pattern is

$$P'(S) = \frac{1}{\lambda} \int_{-\infty}^{\infty} A(x)\, \exp(j(kS + \beta)x)\, dx$$

$$= P(S + \beta/k) \tag{3.46}$$

The new pattern therefore has an identical shape to the original one (on a $\sin \alpha$ scale) but is shifted by $\delta(\sin \alpha) = -\beta/k$. (This is an application of the Fourier shift theorem.) If the first pattern has its main beam peak where

$S = 0$, the second pattern has its peak where $S = -\beta/k$. As an example, if $\beta = \pi/\lambda$, the beam maximum is steered from $\alpha = 0$ to $\alpha = -30°$.

Because the pattern has the same shape on a $\sin \alpha$ scale, its beamwidth is constant on this scale. This is *not* constant on an α scale. Let the beamwidth be 2δ on the $\sin \alpha$ scale, and let the beam steering angle be α_0. Then the beamwidth on an α scale is

$$\alpha_1 - \alpha_2$$

where

$$\sin \alpha_1 = \sin \alpha_0 + \delta$$

$$\sin \alpha_2 = \sin \alpha_0 - \delta$$

Assume that δ is small (a narrow beam), and let $\alpha_1 = \alpha_0 + \epsilon$. Then

$$\sin \alpha_1 = \sin (\alpha_0 + \epsilon) = \sin \alpha_0 \cos \epsilon + \cos \alpha_0 \sin \epsilon$$

$$\approx \sin \alpha_0 + \cos \alpha_0 \cdot \epsilon$$

Then $\delta \approx \epsilon \cdot \cos \alpha_0$, and the beamwidth on an α scale becomes

$$2\delta/\cos \alpha_0$$

The beamwidth therefore increases as the steering angle increases. Physically this corresponds to the reduction in projected aperture as the beam is steered (a smaller aperture giving a wider beam).

The principle of beam steering by applying a phase gradient to a radiating aperture is very important, as it allows electronic control of beam direction. This topic will be further discussed in chapters 4 and 6.

3.4 Aperture theory in three dimensions

We now consider the three-dimensional generalisations of the angular spectrum formulae derived in section 3.2, for two dimensions. There the fields had no y dependence, and an aperture of width a was infinitely long in the y direction. We now have an aperture such as shown in figure 3.7, and Cartesian coordinates x, y, z, or spherical polar coordinates r, θ, ϕ, may be appropriate. As in the two-dimensional case, there are two independent polarisations, and we shall give results for the E_x case ($E_y = 0$ in the aperture).

Appendix C gives a detailed account of the steps in the derivation of the formulae quoted below. Comparison between the two-dimensional and three-dimensional results shows a close relationship.

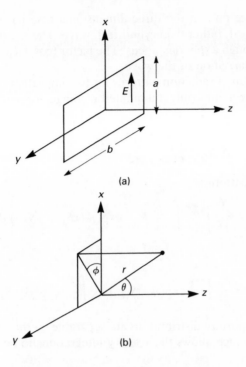

Figure 3.7 (a) Uniform rectangular aperture. (b) Coordinate system

The two-dimensional and three-dimensional radiation patterns of linear and planar apertures are

$$P(S) = \frac{1}{\lambda} \int_{-\infty}^{\infty} E_x(x, 0) \exp(jkxS) \, dx \qquad (3.47)$$

$$P(S_1, S_2) = \frac{1}{\lambda^2} \int_{-\infty}^{\infty} \int_{-\infty}^{\infty} E_x(x, y, 0) \exp(jk(xS_1 + y\, S_2)) \, dx \, dy$$

where $S_1 = \sin\theta \cos\phi$, $S_2 = \sin\theta \sin\phi$, using conventional spherical polar coordinates as in figure 3.7.

In the far field, in two-dimensions and three-dimensions respectively:

$$E = \sqrt{\left(\frac{\lambda}{r}\right)} \cdot \exp(-j(kr - \pi/4)) \, \hat{\boldsymbol{u}}_\theta \, P(\sin\theta). \qquad (3.48)$$

$$E(r, \theta, \phi) = \frac{\lambda}{r} \cdot \exp(-j(kr - \pi/2)) (\cos\phi \hat{\boldsymbol{u}}_\theta - \sin\phi \cos\theta \hat{\boldsymbol{u}}_\phi)$$

$$\times P(S_1, S_2)$$

The dependence on r in the three-dimensional case has now changed to that of a spherical, rather than cylindrical, wave. The $\pi/2$ phase shift is half the π shift through a spherical focus. The factor $(\cos\phi\hat{u}_\theta - \sin\phi\cos\theta\hat{u}_\phi)$ defines the polarisation of the wave.

The evaluation of radiation patterns for two important cases can now be made. Consider a uniformly illuminated rectangular aperture, as in figure 3.7, such that

$$E_x(x, y, 0) = \begin{cases} E_0, & |x| < a/2, \quad |y| < b/2 \\ 0, & \text{elsewhere} \end{cases} \tag{3.49}$$

The radiation pattern is

$$P(S_1, S_2) = \frac{1}{\lambda^2} \int_{-b/2}^{+b/2} \int_{-a/2}^{+a/2} E_0 \cdot \exp(jk(xS_1 + yS_2))\, dx\, dy \tag{3.50}$$

$$= \frac{E_0}{\lambda^2} \int_{-a/2}^{+a/2} \exp(jkx\, S_1)\, dx \cdot \int_{-b/2}^{+b/2} \exp(jky\, S_2)\, dy$$

(Some simple aperture distributions are separable — that is, $E_x(x, y, 0) = E_1(x) \cdot E_2(y)$, which allows the x and y integrations to be separated as in this case.)

Then

$$P(S_1, S_2) = \frac{abE_0}{\lambda^2} \frac{\sin\left(\dfrac{ka}{2} S_1\right)}{\dfrac{ka}{2} S_1} \cdot \frac{\sin\left(\dfrac{kb}{2} S_2\right)}{\dfrac{kb}{2} S_2} \tag{3.51}$$

If $\phi = 0$, $S_1 = \sin\theta$, $S_2 = 0$, and the pattern in the x–z plane is

$$P(S_1, 0) = \frac{abE_0}{\lambda^2} \cdot \frac{\sin\left(\dfrac{ka}{2}\sin\theta\right)}{\dfrac{ka}{2}\sin\theta} \tag{3.52}$$

Also, if $\phi = \pi/2$, $S_1 = 0$, $S_2 = \sin\theta$, and the pattern in the y–z plane is

$$P(0, S_2) = \frac{abE_0}{\lambda^2} \cdot \frac{\sin\left(\dfrac{kb}{2}\sin\theta\right)}{\dfrac{kb}{2}\sin\theta} \tag{3.53}$$

These patterns are of the same form as for a uniform aperture in two dimensions (figure 3.5).

Note that the first zero in the x–z plane is where $\sin \theta = \pm \lambda/a$, and the first zero in the y–z plane is where $\sin \theta = \pm \lambda/b$. The beamwidths in the two principal planes are separately controlled by the aperture dimensions in each plane.

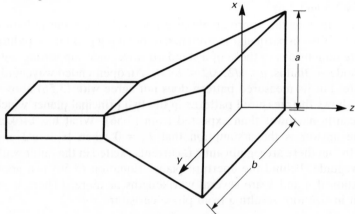

Figure 3.8 Horn antenna

Figure 3.8 shows an electromagnetic horn antenna. A rectangular waveguide supporting the TE_{10} mode (there are also circular equivalents) leads into a region where the walls flare gradually out to end in a larger aperture. The assumption made here is that the field distribution over the radiating aperture is approximately the same as it would be there if the horn did not terminate, but continued as a guide with those dimensions. Any curvature of the wavefront due to limited flare length is also assumed to be negligible — in practice the flare length required increases as the square of the final aperture dimension (compare the Rayleigh distance $2d^2/\lambda$). This requirement makes horns an impractical way of realising very large apertures and hence very directive beams; reflector antennas (see below) are used in such cases. With a gradual flare, the TE_{10} mode distribution is maintained, but expanded to fill the aperture, that is

$$E_x(x, y, 0) = \begin{cases} E_0 \cos(\pi y/b), & |x| < a/2, \quad |y| < b/2 \\ 0, & \text{otherwise} \end{cases} \tag{3.54}$$

The radiation pattern of the horn shown in figure 3.8 is then:

$$P(S_1, S_2) = \frac{E_0}{\lambda^2} \int_{-b/2}^{+b/2} \int_{-a/2}^{+a/2} \cos\left(\frac{\pi y}{b}\right) \exp(jk(xS_1 + yS_2)) \, \mathrm{d}x \, \mathrm{d}y \tag{3.55}$$

This is again separable, with the two integrals similar to the two-dimensional examples given earlier. Thence

$$P(S_1, S_2) = \frac{E_0 ab}{\lambda^2} \cdot \frac{\sin(kaS_1/2)}{kaS_1/2} \cdot \frac{\pi/2 \cos(kbS_2/2)}{\pi^2/4 - k^2 b^2 S_2^2/4} \tag{3.56}$$

In the x–z plane ($S_2 = 0$), the first zero of the pattern is where $\sin \theta = \lambda/a$, whereas in the y–z plane ($S_1 = 0$), the first zero is where $\sin \theta = 3/2 \; \lambda/b$. The sidelobes in the y–z plane are at a lower level than in the x–z plane. (See figures 3.5 and 3.6)

There are limits to the approximations made in deriving the radiation pattern above. One in particular is stretched to breaking point if we reduce the aperture dimensions to those of a standard waveguide supporting only the TE_{10} mode — that is, $a < \lambda/2$, $\lambda/2 < b < \lambda$. An open-ended waveguide does radiate, but its measured pattern does not agree with (3.56) above. Figure 3.9 shows the measured patterns in the two principal planes which are significantly narrower than expected from (3.56). What has broken down? The answer is the assumption that $E_x = 0$ when $|x| > a/2$ and $|y| > b/2$. In fact there are significant r.f. currents excited in the outer walls of the waveguide, behind the aperture plane. Equation (3.56) is a good approximation if a and b are several wavelengths or more. (There is an upper limit in size too, resulting from phase curvature.)

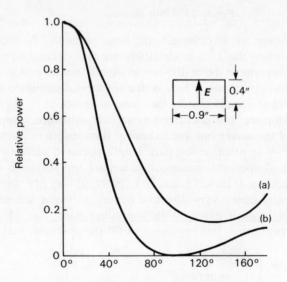

Observed radiation patterns from rectangular waveguide at $\lambda = 3.2$ cm:
(a) *E*-plane pattern; (b) *H*-plane pattern

Figure 3.9 Open-ended waveguide radiation pattern (reproduced, with
        permission, from Jasik, H. (Ed.) *Antenna Engineering Handbook*,
        McGraw-Hill, 1961)

Reflector antennas can also be treated using aperture theory. There are various forms of reflector antenna, and a variety of analysis (and synthesis) techniques applicable to them. Here only the simplest case will be treated, namely a centre-fed paraboloid, shown in figure 3.10. The approximations of geometrical optics will be used to define the aperture distribution. 'Edge diffraction' effects will not be included; these can be important in the 'far out' sidelobe region.

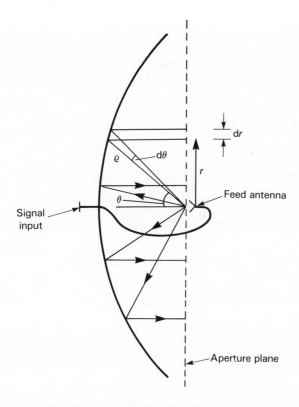

Figure 3.10 Centre-fed paraboloid

The most important property of a parabolic reflector antenna is the equality of path lengths for all rays from a feed antenna at the focus to the aperture plane (via the reflector). The aperture excitation is therefore of uniform phase, as were our previous examples.

The amplitude distribution across the aperture is determined by two factors, the radiation pattern of the feed antenna (typically a horn) and a geometrical factor which depends on f/D, where f is the focal length of the parabola, and D the reflector diameter. This latter factor can be derived as follows. The assumptions of geometrical optics lead to power being conserved within a 'tube' of rays. Thus the power radiated into the cone of angles defined by $d\theta$ in figure 3.10 arrives at the aperture plane in a thin ring of thickness dr.

If the feed antenna's radiation pattern is $F(\theta, \phi)$, then the power density in the aperture plane, $S_a(r)$ is

$$S_a(r) \propto \frac{|F(\theta, \phi)|^2 \cdot 2\pi \sin \theta \, d\theta}{2\pi r dr} \tag{3.57}$$

The parabolic reflector curve can be expressed in (ρ, θ) coordinates as:

$$\rho = 2f/(1 + \cos \theta) = f \sec^2(\theta/2) \tag{3.58}$$

and

$$r = \rho \sin \theta = 2f \tan(\theta/2) \tag{3.59}$$

Then

$$\frac{dr}{d\theta} = f \sec^2(\theta/2) = \rho \tag{3.60}$$

$$S_a(r) \propto |F(\theta, \phi)|^2 \cdot \frac{\sin \theta}{r\rho} = |F(\theta, \phi)|^2 \frac{1}{\rho^2} \tag{3.61}$$

The field distribution in the aperture plane is therefore

$$E_a \propto \frac{F(\theta, \phi)}{\rho} \propto F(\theta, \phi) \cdot \cos^2(\theta/2) \tag{3.62}$$

The factor $\cos^2(\theta/2)$ shows the extra amplitude taper provided by the reflector geometry. For example, if $f/D = 0.25$, such that the focus is in the plane defined by the reflector rim, $\theta_{max} = 90°$, and the 'edge taper' effect is 0.5 in field, that is, -6 dB. For large f/D the effect is small.

The simplest, idealised case for radiation pattern analysis is a feed providing a uniform illumination over a circular aperture. The radiation pattern in any plane is a Bessel function, shown in figure 3.11. The first sidelobe level is -17.6 dB, and the 3 dB beamwidth is $1.02 \, \lambda/D$. The (normalised) pattern function is

$$\frac{2 J_1 (ka \sin \theta)}{ka \sin \theta} \tag{3.63}$$

(where $D = 2a$). If an amplitude taper is superimposed on this field distribution, the beamwidth increases and the sidelobes are (generally) reduced, just as for a linear aperture.

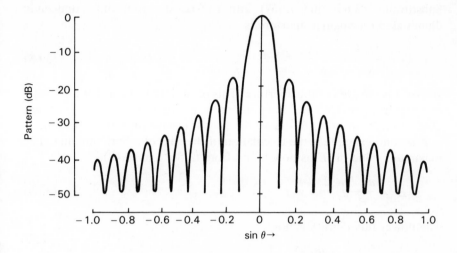

Figure 3.11 Uniform circular aperture radiation pattern (10λ diameter)

3.5 Gain

The concept of antenna gain was introduced in chapter 1. Equation (1.21) can be rearranged as

$$G = \frac{4\pi \, r^2 (P/A)}{P_T} \tag{3.64}$$

Consider the uniformly illuminated rectangular aperture of the previous section, defined by (3.49). Its radiation pattern, $P(S_1, S_2)$, is given by (3.51). The far field, $E(r, \theta, \phi)$, is found from (3.48). The maximum value of E for a given r is found where $S_1 = S_2 = 0$; this value is

$$|E| = \frac{abE_0}{r\lambda} \tag{3.65}$$

The power flux density is

$$P/A = \frac{1}{2} \frac{|E|^2}{Z_0} = \frac{1}{2Z_0} \left(\frac{ab \, E_0}{r\lambda} \right)^2 \tag{3.66}$$

The power transmitted, P_T, is found by *assuming* that $E/H = Z_0$ in the aperture — this is a fair assumption if $a, b \gg \lambda$. Then

$$P_T = \frac{1}{2} \frac{E_0^2}{Z_0} \, ab \tag{3.67}$$

Substituting (3.66) and (3.67) into (3.64), the gain of a uniformly illuminated rectangular aperture is

$$G = \frac{4\pi ab}{\lambda^2} = \frac{4\pi A}{\lambda^2} \tag{3.68}$$

where A is the area of the aperture. This result is in fact true for any shape of aperture, provided the illumination is uniform. Equation (3.68) was used as (1.25) in order to derive the Friis transmission formula (1.28).

A second example is the calculation of the gain of a horn antenna. The maximum value of $|E|$ is now found from (3.56) and (3.48):

$$|E| = \frac{ab\,E_0}{r\lambda} \cdot \frac{2}{\pi} \tag{3.69}$$

The power flux density is now

$$P/A = \frac{1}{2Z_0} \cdot \left(\frac{abE_0}{r\lambda}\right) \cdot \frac{4}{\pi^2} \tag{3.70}$$

The power transmitted, again using the assumption $E/H = Z_0$, is

$$\begin{aligned}
P_T &= \frac{1}{2} \frac{E_0^2}{Z_0} a \int_{-b/2}^{+b/2} \cos^2(\pi y/b)\, dy \\
&= \frac{1}{2} \frac{E_0^2}{Z_0} \frac{ab}{2}
\end{aligned} \tag{3.71}$$

The gain now becomes

$$G = \frac{4\pi ab}{\lambda^2} \cdot \frac{8}{\pi^2} \tag{3.72}$$

Compared with the uniformly illuminated aperture case, the maximum power flux density is multiplied by $4/\pi^2$; however the power transmitted is multiplied by $\frac{1}{2}$ so the net gain is $8/\pi^2$ times that for the uniform aperture. The effective area (see equation (1.26)) is therefore ≈ 80 per cent of the geometrical area for a horn antenna. The 'aperture efficiency' of aperture type antennas is defined as the ratio of the effective area to the geometrical area. A typical figure for a front-fed parabolic reflector antenna is about 55 per cent. Aperture efficiency should not be confused with antenna efficiency, η (equation (1.22)).

3.6 Case study: airport radar antennas

Figure 3.12(a) shows a simple pulse radar system in schematic form (Radar = *Radio Detection and Ranging*). A particular type of waveform — for example, a pulse modulated sine wave — is transmitted, and the echo signal detected. One common or two separate antennas can be used. Distance is determined by measuring the time taken to the target and back. Angular position is found by using an antenna with a narrow azimuth beamwidth, rotating mechanically about a vertical axis. A radar display screen shows range on the radial axis and angular position directly. The antenna requirements are thus a narrow beam in azimuth, and a fairly broad beam in elevation. From aperture theory, the antenna therefore requires a large horizontal dimension, and a small vertical dimension. A common form of airport radar antenna is a reflector with an elliptical aperture shape.

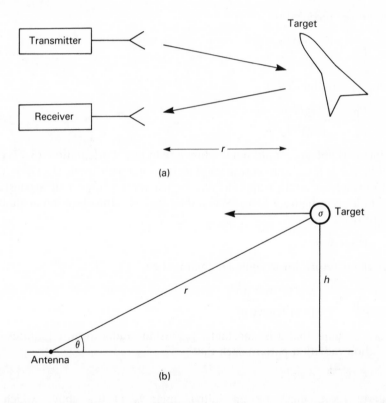

Figure 3.12 (a) Radar system schematic. (b) Aircraft approaching an airport

There is a further consideration for the elevation pattern, which requires a knowledge of the 'radar equation'. Consider figure 3.12(a), and assume that the antennas are pointed towards the target. The power density incident on the target is then

$$S_{\text{inc}} = P/A = \frac{P_T G_T}{4\pi r^2} \tag{3.73}$$

(T ≡ transmit). The power intercepted by the target is

$$P_{\text{inc}} = \sigma S_{\text{inc}} \tag{3.74}$$

where σ is the 'radar cross-section', and is the equivalent area of the target as if the target re-radiated the incident power isotropically. The power density arriving at the receiver is then

$$S_R = \sigma S_{\text{inc}}/(4\pi r^2) \tag{3.75}$$

The power received is

$$P_R = \frac{A_{\text{eR}} \cdot \sigma S_{\text{inc}}}{4\pi r^2} \tag{3.76}$$

Using (1.26) and (3.73)

$$\frac{P_R}{P_T} = \frac{\lambda^2 G_R G_T \sigma}{(4\pi)^3 r^4} \tag{3.77}$$

In fact σ is not a constant, but is a function of target orientation; (3.77) can still be used. If a common transmit/receive antenna is used, $G_R \, G_T \equiv G^2$.

Consider an aircraft approaching or leaving an airport at a constant height h, as in figure 3.12(b). When the range is r, the elevation angle θ is found from

$$\text{cosec } \theta = r/h \tag{3.78}$$

The radar return for a single antenna is then

$$P_R/P_T = \frac{\lambda^2 \{G(\theta)\}^2 \sigma h^4}{(4\pi)^3 (\text{cosec } \theta)^4} \tag{3.79}$$

If we assume that σ is constant, a constant radar return requires an elevation radiation pattern such that

$$G(\theta) \propto \text{cosec}^2\theta \tag{3.80}$$

Clearly there must be an initial angle θ_0 (> 0), above which a $\text{cosec}^2\theta$ pattern can be used. A practical elevation pattern has a main beam with its peak at an elevation angle θ_0, and a $\text{cosec}^2\theta$ 'roll-off' for higher elevation angles. Such a pattern can be synthesised using a reflector antenna which is 'shaped', rather than parabolic, in its elevation cross-section.

4 Linear Arrays

4.1 Introduction

In the previous chapter it was shown that the radiation pattern of an aperture antenna is the spatial Fourier transform of the aperture distribution. Antenna radiation patterns can therefore, in principle, be synthesised by control of the aperture excitation. If the aperture excitation can also be varied electronically, an adaptable radiation pattern is available. Electronic beam steering or null steering (to minimise interference) could therefore be provided. There are limitations on beamwidth imposed by the aperture size, as the Fourier transform relationship implies. In practice, it is very difficult to implement control of the excitation of a continuous aperture. An array antenna allows far more control by using a number of individual antenna elements grouped together to form a sampled aperture. The array elements themselves may not be very much more expensive than a continuous aperture antenna (such as a reflector), but in general the control devices are a significant cost penalty. This has to be traded off against the various advantages of an array antenna system.

Because an array is a *sampled* aperture, there are limitations on the spacing of the array elements. A typical spacing is of the order of $\lambda/2$ (this will be explained below), and so fairly small antennas are required as elements. Dipoles, monopoles, slots, patches and open-ended waveguides can all be used.

The theory given in this chapter will be for a linear array of identical, equispaced elements. This is the simplest case, and is also commonly used in practice. The effects of mutual coupling between elements will be ignored in this chapter. (Chapter 6 will give a brief introduction.) It will be assumed that individual phase and amplitude control of each element is available. There are various ways of implementing this control, and some of these will be explained in chapter 6.

4.2 The radiation pattern of a linear array

Figure 4.1 shows a linear array of equispaced antenna elements. Firstly we shall consider the radiation pattern of an array of (hypothetical) isotropic radiators, $F(\theta)$. This pattern is called the 'array factor'. Note that the angle θ is now defined relative to the array axis, rather than the normal to the aperture, as in chapter 3. This is because the array line is an axis of symmetry for the array factor, which is then a function of θ only.

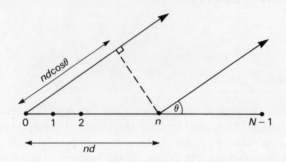

Figure 4.1 Linear array of equispaced antenna elements

The array in figure 4.1 contains N elements with spacing d. In the direction θ the path from the nth element to a distant point is $nd\cos\theta$ shorter than that from the zeroth (reference) element to the same distant point. If the nth element is excited with amplitude $|a_n|$ and phase ϕ_n, the contribution from that element to the field at a great distance at the angle θ is proportional to

$$|a_n| \exp(j\phi_n) \cdot \exp(jn\,kd\cos\theta) \qquad (4.1)$$

The total field is then

$$F = \sum_{n=0}^{N-1} a_n \cdot \exp(jn\,kd\cos\theta) \qquad (4.2)$$

where a_n is a complex number $(= |a_n| \exp(j\phi_n))$. A useful method of analysing linear arrays, due to Schelkunoff, consists of associating a polynomial with an array. Let

$$z = \exp(jkd\cos\theta) \qquad (4.3)$$

Then (4.2) becomes

$$F(z) = a_0 + a_1 z + a_2 z^2 + \ldots a_{N-1}\,z^{N-1} \qquad (4.4)$$

The radiation pattern (array factor) is $F(z) = F(\exp(jkd\cos\theta))$. The complex coefficients of the polynomial $F(z)$ are the excitations of the individual elements in the array. In the general case, the form (4.2) is often used directly to evaluate $F(\theta)$.

As an example, consider an array where all the elements are excited with unit amplitude and zero phase. This is the sampled equivalent of a uniformly excited linear aperture. The radiation pattern for N elements is

$$F(z) = 1 + z + z^2 + \ldots + z^{N-1}$$

$$= (1 - z^N) / (1 - z)$$

$$= \frac{1 - \exp(jkdN \cos \theta)}{1 - \exp(jkd \cos \theta)} \tag{4.5}$$

Then

$$|F(z)|^2 = F(z) \cdot F^*(z) = \frac{2 - 2\cos(Nkd \cos \theta)}{2 - 2\cos(kd \cos \theta)} = \frac{\sin^2(\tfrac{1}{2} Nkd \cos \theta)}{\sin^2(\tfrac{1}{2} kd \cos \theta)}$$

$$|F(z)| = \frac{\sin(\tfrac{1}{2} Nkd \cos \theta)}{\sin(\tfrac{1}{2} kd \cos \theta)} \tag{4.6}$$

Figure 4.2 shows the function $\sin Nx / N \sin x$ (with $N = 10$). This is a normalised form (peak value of unity) for (4.6) if

$$x = \tfrac{1}{2} kd \cos \theta = \frac{\pi d}{\lambda} \cos \theta \tag{4.7}$$

The result (4.6) can be compared with the radiation pattern of a uniform aperture of length a:

$$P(\sin \alpha) = \frac{\sin(\tfrac{1}{2} ka \sin \alpha)}{(\tfrac{1}{2} ka \sin \alpha)} \tag{4.8}$$

The numerator is exactly the same if $a = Nd$, noting that $\sin \alpha = \cos \theta$. The denominators differ, but are similar if

$$\sin(\tfrac{1}{2} kd \cos \theta) \approx \tfrac{1}{2} kd \cos \theta$$

that is

$$\tfrac{1}{2} kd \cos \theta \ll \pi/2$$

$$d \cos \theta \ll \lambda/2 \tag{4.9}$$

(They also differ by a factor N, but that is simply a constant of proportionality.) If $d = \lambda/2$, this condition requires $\cos \theta \ll 1$, so that the patterns are similar near broadside to the aperture or array. The zero-to-zero beamwidth is the same for the two cases. In general, the pattern is similar to that of a diffraction grating in optics, and the denominator can cause 'grating lobes'. The condition for these is

$$\tfrac{1}{2} kd \cos \theta = \pm \pi$$

$$\cos \theta = \pm \lambda/d \tag{4.10}$$

At such angles, the denominator in (4.6) becomes zero, simultaneous with the numerator, and a repeated main lobe occurs in the array factor radiation pattern. Referring to figure 4.2, the first zeros of the pattern occur where $x = \pi/N$, that is $\cos\theta$ ($\equiv \sin\alpha$) $= \pm\lambda/(Nd)$, while the first grating lobes occur where $x = \pi$, that is, $\cos\theta = \pm\lambda/d$. The main beam width is thus governed by the complete array length, while the grating

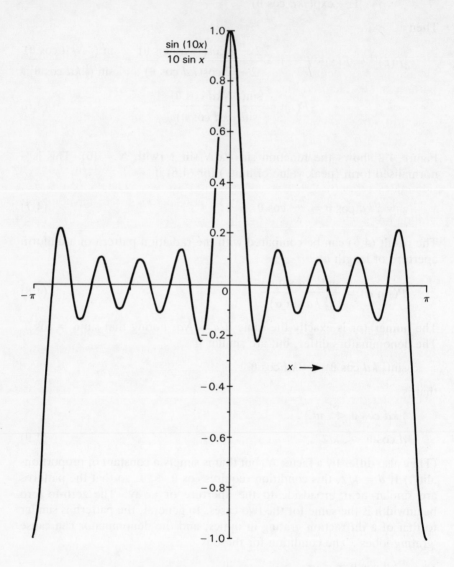

Figure 4.2 The function $\sin(Nx)/N\sin x$ (with $N = 10$)

lobes are governed by the spacing of the array elements. The relation (4.10) implies that, if grating lobes are to be avoided, $d < \lambda$ is required. When beam steering is considered (section 4.5), further restrictions on d occur.

Now consider non-isotropic elements. The radiation pattern now becomes

$$F(\theta, \phi) = \sum_{n=0}^{N-1} a_n \cdot f_n(\theta, \phi) \cdot \exp(jnkd \cos \theta) \qquad (4.11)$$

Here $f_n(\theta, \phi)$ is the radiation pattern of the nth array element. If the array elements have identical patterns, and similar alignment, the element pattern can be factored out, so that

$$F(\theta, \phi) = f(\theta, \phi) \cdot \sum_{n=0}^{N-1} a_n \cdot \exp(jnkd \cos \theta) \qquad (4.12)$$

This is simply the product of the element pattern and the array factor. The array factor is generally more directive than the element pattern, so that it dominates properties such as main beamwidth and sidelobe levels. The element pattern will generally reduce far out sidelobe levels, including any grating lobes which may be present.

4.3 Nulls

A null of the radiation pattern is here taken to be synonymous with a zero — that is, no transmission or reception at a particular angle. A null can also mean a minimum of the pattern, but in the present analysis exact zeros can be achieved. The analysis and synthesis of nulls can be achieved using Schelkunoff's representation.

Consider the complex variable:

$$z = \exp(jkd \cos \theta) \qquad (4.13)$$

As θ varies from 0 to π, z moves along a locus in the Argand diagram, as shown in figure 4.3. The modulus of z is 1, while its phase (argument) is

$$\frac{2\pi d}{\lambda} \cos \theta$$

which therefore varies between $-2\pi d/\lambda$ and $+2\pi d/\lambda$. The locus of z is therefore an arc of the unit circle in the Argand diagram. For a large value of d, z may move several times round the unit circle as θ varies from 0 to π. If $d = \lambda/2$, the locus of z as θ varies from 0 to π just closes to form a complete circle. If $d \ll \lambda/2$ the locus of z is a small arc of the unit circle.

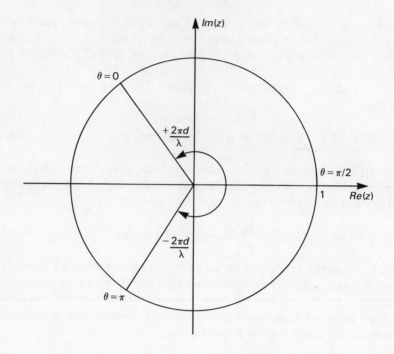

Figure 4.3 Argand diagram for $z = \exp(jkd \cos \theta)$

Now consider the polynomial representation (4.4). Any polynomial can be expressed as a product of linear factors. The polynomial (4.4) will have $N-1$ roots $z_1, z_2 \ldots z_{N-1}$, and it can be written:

$$F(z) = a_{N-1} (z - z_1) (z - z_2) \ldots (z - z_{N-1})$$

Since only the relative radiation pattern is important, we can set $a_{N-1} = 1$, and then

$$F(z) = (z - z_i) (z - z_2) \ldots (z - z_{N-1}) \qquad (4.14)$$

The roots z_1, z_2, etc. (of $F(z) = 0$) are complex numbers, but do not necessarily lie on the unit circle. If they do lie on the unit circle, *and d* is such that that part of the unit circle is traversed by z as θ varies from 0 to π, a null will be present in the radiation pattern. As there are $N-1$ roots for an N element array, there can be up to $N-1$ independent nulls. The use of equation (4.14) in analysis and synthesis can be shown by some simple examples.

Example 1

A three-element array has excitations 1, 1 and −2. Then

$$F(z) = 1 + z - 2z^2$$
$$= (1 + 2z)(1 - z) \qquad (4.15)$$

The roots are $z_1 = 1$, $z_2 = -\frac{1}{2}$. Figure 4.4(a) shows the Argand diagram. For any spacing d, there is a null when $\theta = \pi/2$ ($z = 1$). There are no other independent nulls. The $\theta = \pi/2$ (broadside) result is obvious by inspection, but we have proved that there are no other nulls (for $d < \lambda$). If, however, $d \geqslant \lambda$, the locus of z traverses the unit circle twice, and extra nulls, analogous to grating lobes, appear from the one root z_1.

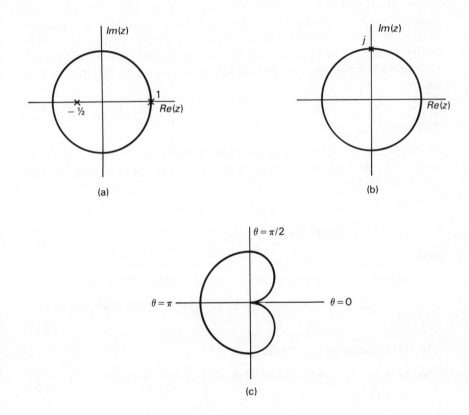

(a)

(b)

(c)

Figure 4.4 (a) Argand diagram for example 1. (b) Argand diagram for example 2. (c) Radiation pattern for example 2 with $d = \lambda/4$

Example 2

A two-element aray has excitations 1 and j (that is, equal amplitudes but with a 90° phase difference). Now

$$F(z) = 1 + jz \tag{4.16}$$

and $z_1 = j$. Figure 4.4(b) shows the Argand diagram. The radiation pattern contains a null if $d > \lambda/4$. The angular position of the null is found from

$$\exp(jkd \cos \theta) = z_1 = j \tag{4.17}$$

whence

$$\frac{2\pi d}{\lambda} \cos \theta = \pi/2 + 2\pi n \tag{4.18}$$

If $d = \lambda/4$, $\cos \theta = 1$ ($\theta = 0$) is the only solution (the $2\pi n$ allows for multiple traverses of the unit circle if d is large enough). The radiation pattern is then a cardioid shape, shown in figure 4.4(c). This array configuration can be used as a simple homing system: a minimum signal is received when the two array elements are in line with the transmitting source.

Example 3

A four-element array is to provide a radiation pattern with nulls at $\theta = 45°$, 90° and 135°. (This is now a synthesis rather than an analysis problem). Here:

$$z_1 = \exp(jkd \cos \theta_1) = \exp(jkd/\sqrt{2})$$
$$z_2 = 1, z_3 = \exp(-jkd/\sqrt{2})$$

and

$$F(z) = (z - \exp(jkd/\sqrt{2})) \, (z - 1) \, (z - \exp(-jkd/\sqrt{2}))$$
$$= z^3 - z^2(1 + 2 \cos(kd/\sqrt{2})) + z(1 + 2 \cos (kd/\sqrt{2})) - 1$$

$$\tag{4.19}$$

The array coefficients are therefore:

$$a_3 = 1, \quad a_2 = -(1 + 2 \cos(kd/\sqrt{2}))$$
$$a_1 = (1 + 2 \cos(kd/\sqrt{2})), \quad a_0 = -1 \tag{4.20}$$

The coefficients a_i vary with the spacing d, but the nulls always exist; the synthesis starts from θ values and so ensures that the z_i are traversed by the locus of z. The coefficients are all real, and this is due to the symmetry of the radiation pattern about broadside. An array distribution with real coefficients always gives a radiation pattern whose amplitude (modulus) is symmetrical about broadside.

4.4 Pattern multiplication

Consider the polynomial

$$F_a(z) = a_0 + a_1z + a_2z^2 + \ldots a_{N-1}z^{N-1} \tag{4.21}$$

representing the radiation pattern of a particular N element array with inter-element spacing d. Next consider the polynomial

$$F_b(z) = b_0 + b_1z + b_2z^2 + \ldots b_{M-1}z^{M-1} \tag{4.22}$$

representing the radiation pattern of an M element array with inter-element spacing d.

If we wish to synthesise a radiation pattern

$$F_c(z) = F_a(z) \times F_b(z) \tag{4.23}$$

all that is necessary is to multiply the two polynomials, (4.21) and (4.22), and identify the element amplitudes as the coefficients of the resulting polynomial. This will be of order $M + N - 2$, implying an array containing $M + N - 1$ elements. As an example, consider a four element array with equal amplitudes and phases, which has a radiation pattern

$$|F(\cos \theta)| = \frac{\sin(2kd \cos \theta)}{\sin(\tfrac{1}{2} kd \cos \theta)} \tag{4.24}$$

This is approximately of the form $\sin x/x$, and the first sidelobe is ≈ -13 dB. Now say that a pattern of the form $(\sin x/x)^2$ is required, with a first sidelobe ≈ -26 dB. Let

$$F_a(z) = F_b(z) = 1 + z + z^2 + z^3 \tag{4.25}$$

Then consider $F_c(z) = F_a(z) \times F_b(z)$:

$$F_c(z) = 1 + 2z + 3z^2 + 4z^3 + 3z^4 + 2z^5 + z^6 \tag{4.26}$$

Thus, a seven-element array, with a triangular amplitude distribution (cophased), provides a radiation pattern

$$|F_c(\cos \theta)| = \left\{ \frac{\sin(2kd \cos \theta)}{\sin(\tfrac{1}{2} kd \cos \theta)} \right\}^2 \tag{4.27}$$

For a continuous linear aperture distribution as in section 3.2, a triangular distribution has a Fourier transform proportional to $(\sin x/x)^2$.

The above example is an illustration of amplitude tapers. The tapered distribution of $F_c(z)$ gives lower sidelobes than a uniform distribution. The patterns (4.24) and (4.27) have the same zero-to-zero beamwidths, but (4.27) comes from a seven-element, rather than a four-element, array. Effectively the beamwidth has increased, as expected when an amplitude taper is applied.

4.5 Beam steering

Consider a general array excitation a_n $(n = 0, 1, \ldots N-1)$. The corresponding radiation pattern is

$$F_a(z) = \sum_{n=0}^{N-1} a_n z^n, \text{ where } z = \exp(j\,kd\cos\theta) \qquad (4.28)$$

Now apply a linear phase gradient to the array — that is, let the array excitations become

$$a_0,\ a_1 \exp(j\phi),\ a_2 \exp(j2\phi),\ \text{etc.}$$

Let

$$b_n = a_n \exp(jn\phi) \qquad (4.29)$$

Then the new radiation pattern is

$$F_b(z) = \sum_{n=0}^{N-1} a_n \exp(jn\phi)\, z^n$$

$$= \sum_{n=0}^{N-1} a_n\, (z')^n \qquad (4.30)$$

where

$$z' = \exp(j(kd\cos\theta + \phi)) \qquad (4.31)$$

Then, if

$$kd\cos\theta_b + \phi = kd\cos\theta_a: \qquad (4.32)$$
$$F_b(\cos\theta_b) = F_a(\cos\theta_a)$$

The radiation pattern keeps the same form, but with an angular shift related to the incremental phase ϕ. From (4.32):

$$\cos\theta_b - \cos\theta_a = -\phi/kd \qquad (4.33)$$

The right hand side of (4.33) is proportional to the phase gradient $(d\phi/dx)$ along the array.

If the main beam peak is initially at $\theta = 90°$, broadside to the array, then $\cos\theta_a = 0$, and $\cos\theta_b = \sin\alpha$, where α is the beam deflection angle.

Then

$$\sin \alpha = -\phi/kd \tag{4.34}$$

If $d = \lambda/2$, and α is small so that $\sin \alpha \approx \alpha$, then

$$\alpha \text{ (radians)} \approx -\phi \text{ (radians)}/\pi$$

$$\alpha° \approx -\phi°/\pi \tag{4.35}$$

Thus, for an incremental phase value of 30°, the deflection angle is $\approx 10°$. Using (4.34), an incremental phase of 90° for $\lambda/2$ spaced elements gives a deflection angle of 30°.

The use of electronically controlled phase shifters on each element of a 'phased' array allows the beam-pointing direction of an array antenna to be varied rapidly and without any mechanical movement of the antenna. This is in contrast to a fixed beam antenna, such as a simple horn-fed parabolic reflector, where the antenna is rotated mechanically to 'scan' the beam. However, the latter is in general much cheaper!

The question of grating lobes arose in section 4.2, where $d < \lambda$ was required to avoid them, for a beam with a broadside peak. The radiation pattern of a uniformly excited N element array is

$$|F_a(z)| = \frac{\sin(\frac{1}{2} N \, kd \cos \theta_a)}{\sin(\frac{1}{2} kd \cos \theta_a)}$$

Now consider this array with a phase gradient superimposed. Using equation (4.32):

$$|F_b(z)| = \frac{\sin(\frac{1}{2} N(kd \cos \theta_b + \phi))}{\sin(\frac{1}{2}(kd \cos \theta_b + \phi))} \tag{4.36}$$

The peak of this radiation pattern is at $\theta = \theta_m$, where

$$\cos \theta_m = -\phi/kd \tag{4.37}$$

Equation (4.36) can therefore be written as

$$|F(z)| = \frac{\sin(\frac{1}{2} N \, kd(\cos \theta - \cos \theta_m))}{\sin(\frac{1}{2}kd(\cos \theta - \cos \theta_m))} \tag{4.38}$$

Grating lobes will appear if the denominator of (4.38) becomes zero for some $\theta \neq \theta_m$. This will occur if

$$\cos \theta - \cos \theta_m = \pm \lambda/d \tag{4.39}$$

by comparison with equation (4.10).

Let the deflection angle from broadside ($\theta = 90°$) be α, so that

$$\theta = 90° + \alpha \tag{4.40}$$

Equation (4.39) then becomes

$$\sin \alpha_m - \sin \alpha = \pm \lambda/d \qquad (4.41)$$

The extreme values of $\sin \alpha$ are ± 1. If we consider $\alpha_m > 0$, the magnitude
of the left hand side of (4.41) has a maximum value of

$$\sin \alpha_m + 1 \qquad (4.42)$$

Thus, if

$$\lambda/d > 1 + \sin \alpha_m$$

$$d/\lambda < 1/(1 + \sin \alpha_m) \qquad (4.43)$$

grating lobes will not appear. For example, if the maximum beam steering
angle is 30° from broadside, (4.43) requires $d < 2/3\lambda$. If the beam can be
steered by 90°, to 'end fire', $d < \frac{1}{2}\lambda$ is needed to avoid grating lobes.

4.6 Woodward synthesis of antenna patterns

Woodward (1946) proposed a technique for antenna pattern synthesis
which can be applied to either linear (continuous) apertures or linear
arrays. Before explaining his method, let us consider the Fourier transform
relationship between an aperture excitation and the radiation pattern as a
possible synthesis technique. For a prescribed radiation pattern $F(\sin \alpha)$,
the corresponding linear aperture excitation is

$$E_x(x, 0) = \int_{-\infty}^{\infty} F(\sin \alpha) \exp(-jkx \sin \alpha) \, \mathrm{d}(\sin \alpha)$$

(equation (3.38)). In general, the resulting aperture excitation is of infinite
extent in the x dimension. To use this in practical synthesis requires the
derived $E_x(x, 0)$ to be truncated at finite limits, defined by the edges of the
available aperture. The actual resulting radiation pattern has then to be
found as the Fourier transform of this truncated aperture distribution, and
will differ from the desired pattern. How large the differences are is
dependent on the aperture size and the amount of fine structure in the
desired pattern.

Woodward's synthesis method starts with a known finite aperture
dimension, and allows the desired pattern to be prescribed at a finite
number of discrete angles. The procedure will now be explained, firstly for
a continuous aperture, and secondly for a linear array.

Consider a uniform excitation of a linear aperture of length L, that is

$$f(x, 0) = \begin{cases} 1 & |x| < L/2 \\ 0 & \text{otherwise} \end{cases}$$

which has a radiation pattern

$$P(S) = (L/\lambda) \sin(\pi LS/\lambda)/(\pi LS/\lambda) \tag{4.44}$$

If a linear phase gradient is applied

$$f_1(x, 0) = \begin{cases} \exp(-jkxS_1) & |x| < L/2 \\ 0 & \text{otherwise} \end{cases}$$

the pattern becomes

$$P_1(S) = (L/\lambda) \sin(\pi L(S - S_1)/\lambda)/(\pi L(S - S_1)/\lambda) \tag{4.45}$$

The sin x/x function has the important property of equal spacing (in x) between the peak at $x = 0$ and the zeros at $x = \pm n\pi$ ($n = 1,2,...$). (This property is used in digital communications to minimise inter-symbol interference.) We can therefore construct a set of patterns with steering angles S_i such that each main beam peak coincides with zeros of all the other patterns. Each pattern is of the form (4.45), and

$$S_{i+1} - S_i = \lambda/L \tag{4.46}$$

The synthesis procedure consists of specifying (sampling) the desired pattern $F(S)$ at values of S with spacing $\Delta S = \lambda/L$. Each sampling point is associated with one sin x/x function, and the value $F(S_i)$ gives the (complex) amplitude for that function. The synthesised pattern becomes

$$F_s(S) = \sum_i F(S_i) \frac{\sin(\pi L(S - S_i)/\lambda)}{\pi L(S - S_i)/\lambda} \tag{4.47}$$

It can be seen from (4.47) that $F_s(S) = F(S)$ when S equals any of the S_i. For values of S between the S_i, the pattern $F_s(S)$ will be a continuous function, but cannot be prescribed. Any fine structure of a desired pattern between sampling points will not be reproduced. This is basic to the Fourier transform relationship between an aperture of limited length and its radiation pattern.

The aperture excitation which produces the radiation pattern $F_s(S)$ is

$$f(x, 0) = \sum_i F(S_i) \cdot (\lambda/L) \cdot \exp(-jkx S_i) \tag{4.48}$$

from (4.45) and (4.47).

As an example, a linear aperture of length 10λ gives $\Delta S = 0.1$, giving a maximum of 20 samples between $S = -1$ and $S = +1$ (for example, taking S_i as $-0.95, -0.85 ... +0.95$).

Now consider a linear array of N elements, with uniform spacing, d. The desired array factor is prescribed. (This can be found by dividing the desired overall radiation pattern by the array element pattern). For a uniform excitation of the array (the element excitations $a_n = 1$):

$$P(S) = \sin(\pi L\, S/\lambda)/\sin(\pi d\, S/\lambda) \qquad (4.49)$$

where $L = Nd$. with a linear phase gradient applied

$$a_n = \exp\{-jnkd\, S_i\}$$

the beam peak is steered to $S = S_i$. Here the nth element is located at $x = nd$, with $-L/2 < x < L/2$. The values of n are $-(N-1)/2, -(N-3)/2 \ldots +(N-1)/2$. For example, if $N = 10$, $n = -4\frac{1}{2}, -3\frac{1}{2}, \ldots +4\frac{1}{2}$.

The main beam peak and the zeros of the pattern are again equally spaced, with $\Delta S = \lambda/L$. A similar procedure to the continuous aperture case can therefore be used. The synthesised pattern is

$$F_s(S) = \sum_i F(S_i) \frac{\sin\{\pi L(S - S_i)/\lambda\}}{N \sin\{\pi d(S - S_i)/\lambda\}} \qquad (4.50)$$

and the required array excitation is

$$a_n = \sum_i F(S_i) \cdot \frac{1}{N} \cdot \exp(-jnkd\, S_i) \qquad (4.51)$$

A particular case is now given as an example. The desired array factor pattern is a uniform sector coverage between $\pm 30°$ from broadside, as shown in figure 4.5(a). A ten element array with $\lambda/2$ spacing is to be used. The sampling interval $\Delta S = \lambda/(Nd) = 0.2$. The sampling points are shown in figure 4.5(a). The element excitations are found from (4.51), and are shown in figure 4.5(b). The distribution resembles a truncated $\sin x/x$ function, as one might expect. The synthesised pattern $F_s(S)$ is shown in figure 4.5(c). The finite edge slopes are limited by the size of the aperture in wavelengths.

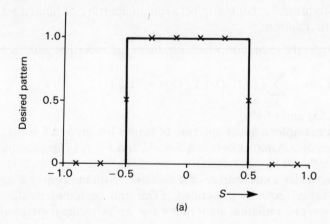

(a)

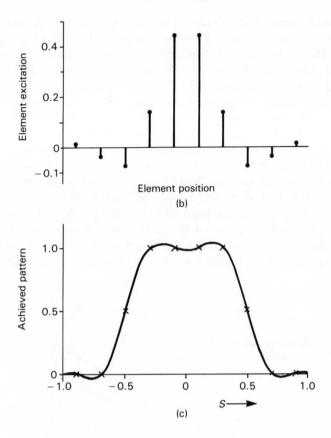

Figure 4.5 (a) Desired sector coverage pattern. (b) Element excitations.
(c) Synthesised pattern

Woodward synthesis is generally used for main beam shaping. Taylor synthesis (Taylor, 1955) can be used if the near-in sidelobe levels need to be controlled.

4.7 Case study: the ILS array system

The Instrument Landing System (ILS) is installed at airfields to allow 'blind' landing. Signals are transmitted from antenna arrays on the ground, and received on an aircraft using a simple antenna. A short vertical array provides signals giving elevation information, and a long horizontal array provides signals giving azimuth information. We shall concentrate on the horizontal array, for which a frequency ≈ 110 MHz is used. The full

Introduction to Antennas

system uses a linear antenna array of length approximately 50 metres and height up to 5 metres, placed laterally beyond the end of the airport runway. The array contains typically 25 antenna elements, radiating horizontal polarisation. Figure 4.6(a) shows one type of element which has been used, a horizontal dipole with a 'corner' reflector.

Two distinct radiation patterns are produced by the array, using two different array excitations. With a single array, these excitations are superimposed (in the antenna distribution unit). Different modulations are used for the two excitations. Figure 4.6(b) shows how the two signals, here called A and B, are fed to the antenna array. Excitation A is symmetrical; excitation B is antisymmetrical, and its phase relative to the excitation for A is +90° in one half of the array, and −90° in the other half.

On the runway centre line (normal to the array), the antisymmetrical excitation gives a null for signal B. To one side of the centre line, the radiation pattern for excitation B is in phase with the pattern for excitation A, while on the other side, the patterns are in antiphase (see explanation

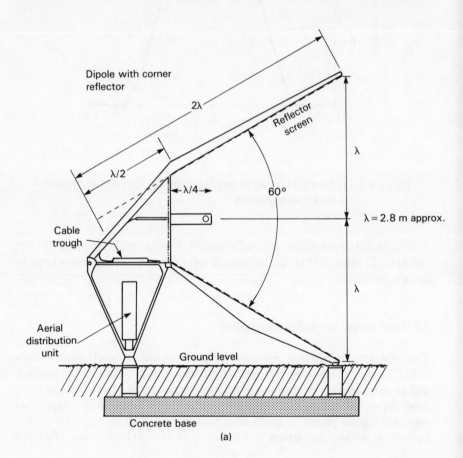

(a)

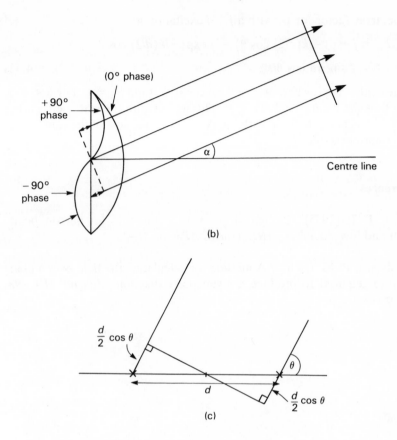

Figure 4.6 The ILS array system: (a) array element; (b) array excitations; (c) two-element array representation

below). By comparing the A and B signals received, the aircraft system can provide the pilot with an indication of which side of the centre line he is, and the angular displacement. The pilot can then correct the flight path to align the aircraft with the runway.

The phase relationships quoted above can be understood by considering a two-element array with symmetrical (A) or antisymmetrical (B) excitations. Figure 4.6(c) shows the geometry, with phases referred to the centre of the array. The array factor for A, with a 1, 1 excitation is

$$F_A = \exp\{-jk(d/2) \cos \theta\} + \exp\{+jk(d/2) \cos \theta\}$$

$$= 2 \cos(\pi d \cos \theta / \lambda) \tag{4.52}$$

The array factor for B, with a j, $-j$ excitation is

$$F_B = j \exp\{-jk(d/2) \cos \theta\} - j \exp\{+jk(d/2) \cos \theta\}$$

$$= 2 \sin(\pi d \cos \theta / \lambda) \tag{4.53}$$

The centre line is where $\theta = \pi/2$, so $\cos \theta = 0$ and $F_B = 0$. For $\theta < \pi/2$, $F_B > 0$, while for $\theta > \pi/2$, $F_B < 0$. This agrees with the statement earlier that the B signal is in phase with the A signal to one side of the centre line, and in antiphase on the other.

References

Taylor, T. T. (1955). 'Design of line source antennas for narrow beam-width and low sidelobes', *IRE Trans.*, *AP3*, pp.16–28.

Woodward, P. M. (1946). 'A method for calculating the field over a plane aperture required to produce a given polar diagram', *Journal IEE*, *93*, pp.1554–8.

5 Antenna Measurements

5.1 Introduction

The main parameters which are used to characterise an antenna are (a) input impedance; (b) radiation pattern (sometimes called a 'polar diagram'), (c) gain, and (d) polarisation.

Experimental evaluation of antennas has several functions. Theoretical predictions may have been made, but usually include approximations, so that measurements can find the detailed differences between theory and experiment. The construction techniques and materials used need to be tested; for example, surface profile inaccuracies in a reflector antenna can lead to a reduction in gain from the ideal, and can increase sidelobe levels at angles dependent on the scale size of the irregularities. Theoretical predictions may not be available for particular antenna structures, and empirical development work can use a series of measurements to refine a design.

Antenna measurements need to be made with the antenna (a) free to radiate, and (b) in a situation representative of its operational use. For example, the radiation pattern of an antenna on an aircraft is dependent on its siting, so the aircraft or at least part of its structure, is an important factor. It is usually impractical to make a comprehensive evaluation of antennas on large structures at full scale, so reduced scale modelling is often employed. Then the linear dimensions of an antenna and its supporting structure (say the aircraft above) are reduced by a factor n, while the operating frequency is increased by n. (The size in wavelengths is therefore unchanged.) Maxwell's equations are invariant under these circumstances, provided that the permittivity and permeability of any dielectric materials used have not changed, and that the conductivity has increased in proportion to the frequency. (The complex permittivity contains a term σ/ω.) If the structure is made of good conductors (as is usually desirable), scale modelling gives a very good representation. Losses are generally more difficult to model.

5.2 Input impedance

An antenna is usually fed via a coaxial cable or other form of transmission line, and a 50Ω characteristic impedance is usually taken as standard.

77

(Domestic antenna cables are, however, 75Ω.) The fraction of power reflected by the antenna is

$$P_{refl}/P_{inc} = |\Gamma|^2 = \left|\frac{Z_{in} - Z_o}{Z_{in} - Z_o}\right|^2 \tag{5.1}$$

where Z_{in} is the antenna input impedance, Z_o the line impedance and Γ the voltage reflection coefficient. Z_{in} is a function of frequency, and its variation with frequency, or that of $|\Gamma|$, is usually what needs to be found. VSWR (Voltage Standing Wave Ratio) measurements are often used — for example, using a field probe in a slotted line at microwave frequencies. The reflection coefficient can then be found from

$$VSWR = V_{max}/V_{min} = (1 + |\Gamma|)/(1 - |\Gamma|) \tag{5.2}$$

If a swept frequency network analyser is available (covering the frequency band of interest), input impedance measurements over a band can be readily made. The network analyser measures the complex reflection coefficient (as a function of frequency), and Z_{in} can then be found.

The measured results can be affected by the presence of nearby objects which can perturb the antenna's reactive field or reflect its radiated field back to it. Moving the antenna by $\lambda/4$ and remeasuring can indicate the presence of such effects.

The bandwidth of an antenna can be defined in terms of a variation in any of its measurable properties. Input impedance is often the limiting factor for useful antenna performance, so the impedance bandwidth is an important parameter. The 3 dB points for this are the frequencies for which $|\Gamma|^2 = \frac{1}{2}$.

5.3 Radiation patterns

Measurements of the 'far field' radiation pattern are usually required. In general

$$E = E(r, \theta, \phi) \tag{5.3}$$

but as $r \to \infty$, E tends to

$$f(\theta, \phi) \cdot \frac{\exp(-jkr)}{r} \cdot \hat{v} \tag{5.4}$$

where $f(\theta, \phi)$ is the (complex) radiation pattern and $\hat{v}$ the polarisation vector (of unit length).

Figure 5.1(a) shows the standard spherical polar coordinate system. Usually only the amplitude radiation pattern $|f(\theta, \phi)|$ is measured. The polarisation vector has two independent components (in the far field), for

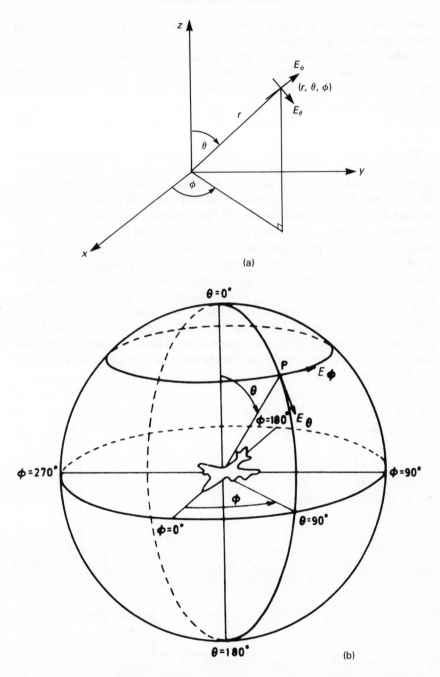

Figure 5.1 (a) Spherical polar coordinate system. (b) Aircraft antenna
coordinates

example $\hat{u}_\theta$ and $\hat{u}_\phi$. In general, two radiation patterns are measured, for two independent polarisations.

Radiation pattern measurements are often made by rotating the antenna under test about a selected axis. This gives a plane cut through the full pattern. A number of such cuts at various angles may be needed to characterise the pattern.

Figure 5.1(b) shows an antenna on an aircraft (a scale model would normally be used). A basic set of pattern cuts is (a) the azimuth $(x-y)$ plane, (b) the roll $(y-z)$ plane, and (c) the pitch $(x-z)$ plane. Typically 'vertical' (V) and 'horizontal' (H) polarisations are used, defined relative to the plane of rotation as horizontal. Thus, for the azimuth plane cut, $E_V \equiv E_\theta$ and $E_H \equiv E_\phi$. However, in the roll and pitch planes, E_V and E_H are not E_θ or E_ϕ, nor do they bear a fixed relation to them.

Figure 5.2 shows a typical equipment configuration for radiation pattern measurements. For plane pattern cuts, rotation about a vertical axis can be used, with the antenna under test supported above the turntable in various orientations. For example, if an aircraft model is fixed with its nose pointing straight up, a roll plane cut is obtained. The antenna at the other end of the antenna 'range' can be varied to make measurements for different polarisations. A linearly polarised horn can simply be rotated to give arbitrary angles of linear polarisation. Thanks to reciprocity, the antenna under test can usually be used to transmit or receive, whichever is most convenient.

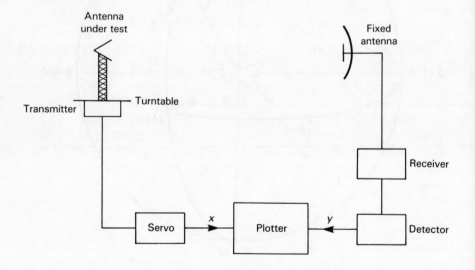

Figure 5.2 Radiation pattern measurement configuration

There are a considerable number of potential error sources in radiation pattern measurements. These include (i) supports and cables attached to the antenna, (ii) finite distance, and (iii) reflections from the ground or surrounding objects.

The antenna needs to be supported above the turntable, and held at various angles for different pattern cuts. The minimum support structure should be used, with materials such as wood, fibre glass or perspex. Support structures can affect the pattern in two ways: (a) by reflection or scattering of the radiation, and/or (b) by directly perturbing the radiation pattern by altering the current distribution on the antenna. Similar considerations apply to connecting cables, which are, unfortunately, normally metallic. Effects due to cables can sometimes be diagnosed by varying the cable run to the antenna. In some cases, it is possible to attach a battery-driven oscillator to the antenna — for example, inside an aircraft model.

In order to obtain accurate far field radiation patterns, the range length R needs to be sufficiently large. Firstly, the antenna under test should be illuminated by a plane wavefront. The simplest way to achieve this is to make

$$R > 2(d_1^2 + d_2^2)/\lambda \tag{5.5}$$

where d_1 is the largest linear dimension of the antenna under test and d_2 is the largest dimension of the other antenna. This is the 'Rayleigh criterion', derived in chapter 1, and this ensures that the phase deviations from a plane wavefront are within $\pm 22\frac{1}{2}°$. An alternative method is adopted in a 'compact range', where d_2 is chosen to be large (using a reflector antenna) such that

$$R \ll 2d_2^2/\lambda$$

and the wavefront is again approximately plane, as in the diffraction picture of section 3.1.

Two other finite distance criteria may need to be considered, particularly at sub-microwave frequencies. The reactive near field is significant within about a wavelength of the antenna, so $R > \lambda$ is required. When an antenna of length d_1 is rotated, the distance from one end to the fixed antenna can vary from $R + \frac{1}{2} d_1$ to $R - \frac{1}{2} d_1$. The l/r field dependence can then give pattern errors. If $\pm \frac{1}{2}$ dB amplitude error is acceptable, $R > 10\, d_1$ is required.

The pattern measurements should be based on the direct signal between the two antennas. Any indirect signal paths, such as a reflection from the ground, create errors in the measured pattern. The radiation patterns of both antennas, 'under test' and 'fixed', are important in assessing the importance of the effect. If a very directive fixed antenna can be used (without violating (5.5)), then we can discriminate against the unwanted reflected signal. The pattern of the antenna under test is also important. When a sidelobe is being measured, the main beam could be producing a relatively large indirect signal. This acts against the discrimination provided by the fixed antenna's pattern. The choice of antenna range geometry to minimise indirect signals is clearly very important.

Two particular geometries are (a) an elevated range, and (b) a vertical range. For (a), both antennas in figure 5.2 are raised high above the ground, using tall buildings, local terrain or masts. Case (b) is shown in figure 5.5, and is discussed in detail as a case study. Both distance and wide angle discrimination against indirect signals are employed in these cases.

At frequencies above about 1 GHz, anechoic chambers can be used. A large room or building has its walls, floor and ceiling lined with RAM (Radio Absorbent Material), which has a very small reflection coefficient for frequencies above a particular value. RAM consists of loaded foam cones, which absorb electromagnetic waves well if their wavelengths $\leq$ cone height. RAM sheets with various cone sizes are available. The lowest measurement frequency required (and the permissible level of reflections) dictates the size used. The main limitation on the use of far field anechoic chambers is the available range length.

A compact range is one way of utilising an anechoic chamber for cases where the Rayleigh distance is long (see above). There is then a defined zone within which the differences in amplitude and phase of the wavefront relative to a plane wave are less than specified limits.

Another important type of antenna range is the 'near field–far field range', again usually using an anechoic chamber. Both amplitude and phase measurements of the near field pattern are made at relatively short range, and then the far field radiation pattern is calculated (on a computer) from these data.

Antenna range performance should be characterised by making measurements on test antennas with known patterns, or by field probing. IEEE (1979) gives details of various test techniques.

5.4 Gain measurements

The Friis transmission formula was obtained in chapter 1, and is

$$P_R/P_T = G_T\, G_R \cdot \left(\frac{\lambda}{4\pi r}\right)^2 \tag{5.6}$$

where power P_T is transmitted by an antenna with gain G_T, and power P_R is received by an antenna with gain G_R. The two antennas are oriented such that the maximum signal is transferred, and polarisation match is assumed. This equation is used as the basis of the three gain measurement methods explained below.

Figure 5.3 shows the comparison method. A standard antenna of known gain is used, where the gain has been established either by previous calibration or by theoretical calculation. The received signal level with the standard antenna is recorded; the unknown is then switched to or substituted, and gain or attenuation inserted to obtain the same level. This then measures the difference in gain.

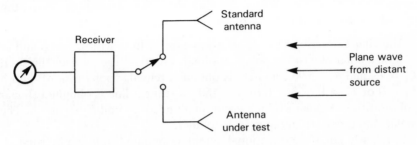

Figure 5.3 Gain comparison

If two identical antennas are used, (5.6) becomes

$$P_R/P_T = \left(\frac{G\lambda}{4\pi r}\right)^2$$

Taking logarithms of both sides:

$$\log(P_T/P_R) = 2\log(r) + 2\log\left(\frac{4\pi}{G\lambda}\right) \tag{5.7}$$

A series of measurements for different values of the spacing r is made, and then $\log(P_T/P_R)$ is plotted against $\log(r)$. This should give a straight line of slope 2 and intercept $2\log(4\pi/G\lambda)$, from which G can be found.

A variant of the above method is to use a plane reflecting sheet in front of a single antenna. The plane reflector is in the far field of the antenna, and is of sufficient area to intercept virtually all of the radiated energy. The ratio P_R/P_T can then be found by a VSWR measurement. The inherent mismatch of the antenna must be allowed for. The plane reflector is oriented so as to maximise the returned signal.

Three antennas with unknown gains G_1, G_2 and G_3 can be used to find all three gains. For one pair:

$$P_R/P_T = \frac{G_1\,G_2\,\lambda^2}{(4\pi r)^2} \tag{5.8}$$

so that G_1G_2 can be found. Similarly, G_2G_3 and G_1G_3 can be measured; then the individual gains can be found by algebraic elimination.

5.5 Polarisation measurements

The polarisation of an electromagnetic wave is in general elliptical (linear and circular are then special cases of the ellipse). For a wave travelling in the z direction, the components E_x and E_y are

$$E_x = E_1 \cos(\omega t - kz)$$
$$E_y = E_2 \cos(\omega t - kz + \delta) \tag{5.9}$$

The shape described by $|E|$ as a function of time with $|E|$ as ρ and ωt as θ on a polar plot (using polar coordinates ρ, θ) is in general an ellipse. If $E_1 = E_2$ and $\delta = \pm 90°$, a circle is obtained (circular polarisation); and if $E_1 = 0$ or $E_2 = 0$ or $\delta = 0$ or $\delta = 180°$, a straight line is obtained (linear polarisation). A polarisation measurement needs to find E_1/E_2 and δ. The 'polarisation pattern' method is as follows.

A linearly polarised directional antenna, mounted so it can be rotated, is connected to a detector calibrated to read relative field intensity. As the linearly polarised antenna is rotated, the signal received from the elliptically polarised antenna is plotted on a polar plot as $P = |E|^2$ *versus* linear polarisation angle, as in figure 5.4. Then

$$P_x/P_y = E_1^2/E_2^2 \tag{5.10}$$

$$\tan 2\tau = \frac{2 E_1 E_2 \cos \delta}{E_1^2 - E_2^2} \tag{5.11}$$

Equation (5.11) can be derived from (5.9) via a stationary value of $|E|^2$.

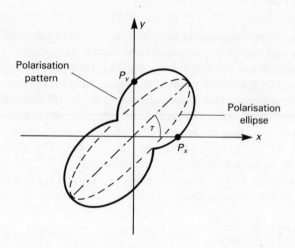

Figure 5.4 Polarisation pattern

5.6 Case study: a vertical antenna range

A vertical antenna range was designed and built specifically for measurements on 1/30 scale models of small aircraft, in the (full scale) frequency range 2–30 MHz (Smith and Nichols, 1978). The actual measurement frequencies were therefore 60–900 MHz. Figure 5.5 shows the general layout of the vertical scale model range, which is 4.6 metres tall. This is about one wavelength at the lowest frequency. A typical length of a small aircraft is 15 metres, so that the scale model has a length d of about 0.5 metres. Pattern errors of $\pm\frac{1}{2}$ dB were considered acceptable.

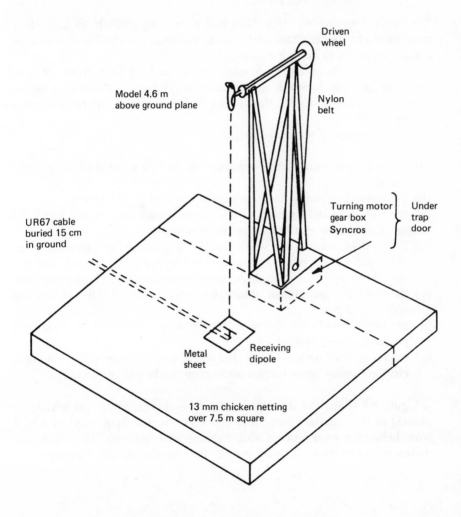

Figure 5.5 Vertical scale model range

Consider the three 'distance' errors discussed in section 5.3. The Rayleigh distance is greatest at the highest frequency, 900 MHz. The range length R therefore needs to satisfy

$$R \geqslant R_1 = 2 \cdot (0.5)^2/0.33 = 1.5 \text{ metres}$$

Reactive field effects are worst at the lowest frequency, 60 MHz, requiring

$$R \geqslant R_2 = \lambda_{max} = 5 \text{ metres}$$

The $1/r$ effects require

$$R \geqslant R_3 = 10 \, d = 5 \text{ metres}$$

The several sources of error described above are unlikely to have their maximum effects simultaneously, so a minimum height for the vertical range was taken to be ≈ 5 metres.

The reactive field criterion may appear to be rather close, $R = \lambda$. However, analysis in Smith and Nichols (1978), using a theoretical model of an aircraft h.f. antenna, shows that the relative pattern errors are still within $\pm\frac{1}{2}$ dB.

Other features of the range include:

(a) no metal parts are in the construction above the level of the ground plane;
(b) the ground screen is flat to within 3 cm ($\lambda/10$ at 900 MHz);
(c) the aircraft model contains a battery-driven oscillator which excites the antenna system at a particular frequency;
(d) the model is rotated in a vertical plane in synchronism with a (remote) polar plotter to obtain a plane cut in the radiation pattern, and the model can be mounted in three positions to give three orthogonal cuts;
(e) the two orthogonal linear polarisations can be provided by rotating the receiving dipole;
(f) the supporting frame can be rotated downwards so that the mounting position is near ground level;
(g) the range is set up in an open area where objects to the side (buildings, etc.) are many times further away then the height of the range.

Figure 5.6 shows the three principal plane cuts (azimuth, pitch and roll planes) of the radiation pattern at 180 MHz (scaled frequency) of a 1/30 scale helicopter model fitted with a strung wire antenna. The rotors are driven round to show the modulating effect on the radiation pattern.

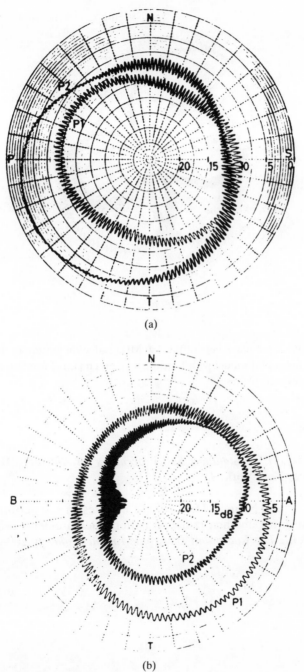

(a)

(b)

Figure 5.6 (continued overleaf)

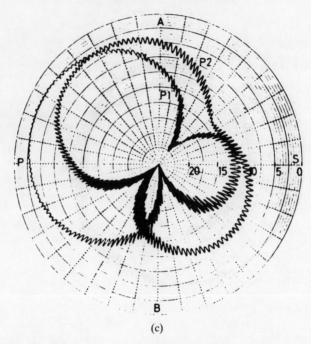

(c)

Figure 5.6 Principal plane cuts of the 180 MHz radiation pattern of a 1/30 scale
helicopter model with a strung wire antenna: (a) azimuth, (b) pitch,
(c) roll, planes

References

IEEE (1979). *IEEE Standard Test Procedures for Antennas*, IEEE/Wiley
Interscience, New York.

Smith, M. S. and Nichols, D. E. T. (1978). 'Design and performance of a
vertical range for antenna radiation pattern measurements using aircraft
scale models', *The Radio and Electronic Engineer*, *48*, pp.209–14.

6 Further Array Topics

6.1 Introduction

In this chapter a selection of more advanced topics is dealt with. These are mainly associated with phased arrays. They are selected because they contain fundamental principles which are not necessarily obvious as extrapolations of the basic theory presented earlier. Phased arrays are an important class of antenna, because they allow electronic control of their aperture excitation. This allows beam shaping, beam steering and null steering. They do however have the major problem of high cost. A number of antenna systems can be devised which do not have the complete flexibility of a fully phased array, but offer some of its advantages at a more reasonable cost. Sections 6.2, 6.3 and 6.4 include some examples of this.

Having dealt only with linear arrays in chapter 4, it is important to consider planar arrays (section 6.4). The effects of mutual coupling in phased arrays are introduced in section 6.5. This places important limits on the beam steering capability of a phased array. Circular arrays are considered in section 6.6.

The 'beam forming' techniques described in this chapter all operate directly at the radio frequency (r.f.). Both intermediate frequency (i.f.) and baseband beam forming can be used (particularly on reception), but such techniques are beyond the scope of this chapter.

6.2 Scanning antennas

A standard phased array consists of a number of antenna elements distributed in space, for example, equispaced along a straight line — a linear array. A single beam is formed by feeding the array elements with the amplitudes and phases needed to create the desired beam shape.

The desired amplitude and phase distribution can be formed using a fixed or variable feed network. Figure 6.1(a) shows a standard configuration for a linear array with a 'corporate' or 'parallel' amplitude distribution network, and a phase shifter for each array element. The power divisions at the junctions may be fixed or variable — the former is usual. In that case, a fixed amplitude distribution results, with corresponding main beam width and sidelobe levels. The phase shifters can then be used to vary the array phase distribution — for example, to steer the beam electronically. The phase shifters are normally composed of a series of discrete valued switched elements (for example, using PIN diodes), although continuously variable units also exist.

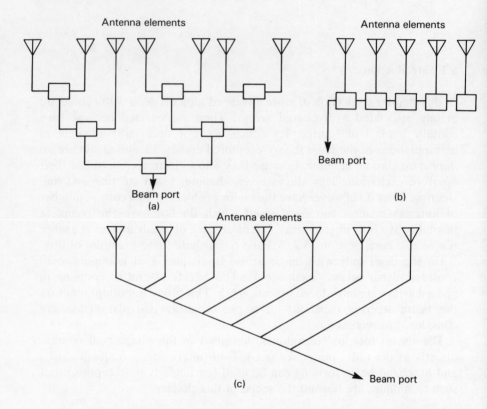

Figure 6.1 (a) Corporate (parallel) feed network. (b) Series feed network. (c) Equal path length, series feed

Figure 6.1(b) shows a 'series' distribution network, where power is progressively coupled out of a feed line into the array elements to give the amplitude distribution. The r.f. path length between successive elements is one wavelength, λ_0, at a particular frequency, f_0 (or $\lambda_0/2$ plus a phase-reversed connection). At that frequency, the array elements are co-phased and a broadside beam is produced. At another frequency f, wavelength λ, there is a phase difference ϕ between elements, given by

$$\phi = 2\pi \left(\frac{\lambda_0}{\lambda} - 1 \right)$$

(6.1)

For a given array spacing d, the beam is then deflected from broadside by an angle α; using equation (4.34):

$$\sin \alpha = -\phi\lambda/(2\pi d) = (\lambda - \lambda_0)/d \tag{6.2}$$

Depending on the application, this effect can either be a benefit or a drawback. A series feed is generally cheaper and requires less space than a parallel feed. 'Frequency scanning', as this effect is called, can be used to steer a beam using a simple (series) feed and no phase shifters. On the other hand, when the communication direction is fixed, the effect can limit the use of a series feed. The deflection angle α is independent of the array length, from equation (6.2); however, the beamwidth reduces as the array is lengthened, so that the deflection becomes a larger fraction of a beamwidth. If the beam is correctly aligned for f_0, it will be misaligned at other frequencies. Once the misalignment is half a beamwidth, the signal level will be down by 3 dB. Clearly this is a significant limitation on either the array length (and hence the beamwidth and gain) or the system bandwidth. A numerical example can be used to illustrate this effect.

Consider an antenna array which has to provide a specific narrow beamwidth. Say that at f_0 (λ_0), the beam points correctly, and this is broadside to the array. Then at $f = f_0 \pm \Delta f/2$, the beam is deflected from broadside by a small angle α, where

$$|\alpha| \approx \left(\frac{\lambda}{\lambda_0} - 1\right) \cdot \frac{\lambda_0}{d} = \left(\frac{f_0}{f} - 1\right) \cdot \frac{\lambda_0}{d} \approx \frac{\Delta f}{f_0} \cdot \frac{\lambda_0}{2d}$$

Let d be $\lambda_0/2$ and the beamwidth be $2°$. Then, if $\alpha = \pm 1°$, there will be a 3 dB reduction in signal at the band edges. Then

$$\Delta f/f_0 \approx \pi/180 \approx 1.8 \text{ per cent}$$

Another type of amplitude distribution network is shown in figure 6.1(c). This is an equal path length, series feed. This does not exhibit frequency scanning, but is less compact than a standard series feed as in figure 6.1(b).

So far we have considered array antennas which are capable of beam scanning over a wide angular sector. If a very narrow, high gain scanned beam is required, a very large phased array could be needed. High gain beams can be readily provided by reflector antennas, but then require mechanical scanning. Figure 6.2 shows a compromise arrangement for 'limited sector scanning'. A small phased array with a wide range of scan angles is combined with an imaging dual reflector to provide a high gain beam scanned over a limited angular sector. The sub-reflector and the main reflector have a common focus. When the array is used to transmit, the sub-reflector aperture distribution is provided by the small array. The imaging arrangement then produces the main reflector aperture distribution. This is a large aperture, and hence a narrow beam is radiated. The phase gradient across the larger aperture is reduced in proportion to the change in aperture size. The scan angle from the main aperture is therefore reduced compared with the scan provided by the small array. The number of beamwidths of scan is maintained; if the main reflector's effective aperture is M times larger than the array aperture, the beamwidth is reduced by a factor of M, but so is the angle of scan.

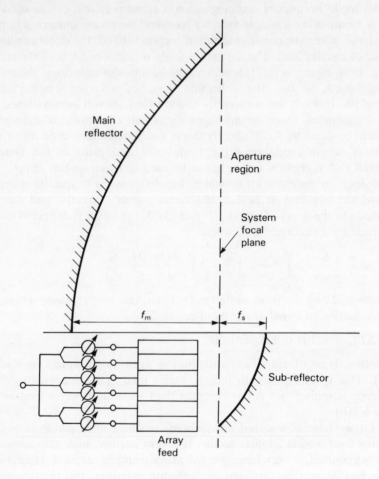

Figure 6.2 Limited sector scanning

6.3 Orthogonal beams and multiple beam formers

Figure 6.3 shows a linear array used in conjunction with a multiple beam former (MBF). The MBF has a number of 'array ports' equal to the number of array elements, and a (not necessarily equal) number of 'beam ports'. The beams formed are in fixed directions (for a given frequency), and are available simultaneously. This means that if, say, a receiver is connected to each beam port, signals can be received from several directions simultaneously.

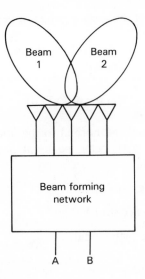

Figure 6.3 Multiple beam former

One simple way of making an MBF is to use power dividers/combiners at each array element, and then have separate distribution networks for each independent beam. This has the disadvantage of being lossy, especially with more than a few beams. It is however used in the ILS array system described in section 4.7.

It is in fact possible to have a lossless (ideally) simultaneous multiple beam former, provided the multiple beams are 'orthogonal'. Orthogonal beams also result in zero mutual coupling between beam ports. Consider figure 6.3. Excitation of port A with unit volts produces a radiation pattern $E_A(\theta)$ and excitation of port B produces pattern $E_B(\theta)$. With both ports excited equally, the radiation pattern will be $E_A(\theta) + E_B(\theta)$. If the MBF is lossless, and there is no coupling between ports A and B, power conservation requires that

$$\int E_A(\theta) \, E_A^*(\theta) \, d\theta + \int E_B(\theta) \, E_B^*(\theta) \, d\theta$$

$$= \int [E_A(\theta) + E_B(\theta)] \, [E_A^*(\theta) + E_B^*(\theta)] \, d\theta \qquad (6.3)$$

The condition for orthogonal beams (that is, no coupling or loss of power) becomes

$$\int E_A(\theta) \, E_B{}^*(\theta) \, d\theta = 0 \tag{6.4}$$

Thus the average value of the cross-product of beam A with the conjugate of beam B must be zero.

Consider an aperture of length L, with an aperture distribution $f(x)$ which produces a radiation pattern

$$E(S = \sin \theta) = \int_{-L/2}^{+L/2} f(x) \, \exp(jkxS) \, dx \tag{6.5}$$

(where θ is the angle from the normal to the aperture). To produce two similarly shaped beams with beam peaks at $S = \pm\sin \alpha$, the necessary aperture distributions are

$$\begin{aligned} g_A(x) &= f(x) \, \exp(jkx \sin \alpha) \\ g_B(x) &= f(x) \, \exp(-jkx \sin \alpha) \end{aligned} \tag{6.6}$$

For the two beams to be orthogonal:

$$\int E_A(S) \, E_B{}^* (S) \, dS = 0 \tag{6.7}$$

(assuming narrow beams so $S = \sin \theta \approx \theta$). Now

$$\begin{aligned} E_A(S) &= \int_{-L/2}^{L/2} f(x) \, \exp(jkx(S + \sin \alpha)) \, dx \\ E_B(S) &= \int_{-L/2}^{L/2} f(y) \, \exp(jky(S - \sin \alpha)) \, dy \end{aligned} \tag{6.8}$$

being careful to use different symbols for the 'dummy' variables x and y. Then (6.7) becomes

$$0 = \int_{-\infty}^{\infty} \int_{-L/2}^{L/2} \int_{-L/2}^{L/2} f(x) \, f^*(y) \, \exp(jkS(x-y)) \, \exp(jk \sin \alpha \, (x+y)) \, dx \, dy \, dS \tag{6.9}$$

Integrating first with respect to S and noting that

$$\int_{-\infty}^{\infty} \exp(juZ) \, du = \delta(Z) \tag{6.10}$$

where $\delta(\ )$ is the Dirac δ function, (6.9) becomes

$$0 = \int_{-L/2}^{L/2} f(x) \, f^*(x) \, \exp(jkx \, 2 \sin \alpha) \, dx \tag{6.11}$$

(The first integration produces $\delta(x-y)$, which is zero when $x \neq y$, and the second integration substitutes x for y in the remaining expression).

The integral (6.11) can be regarded as the radiation pattern corresponding to an aperture distribution equal to the square of the modulus of the basic aperture distribution $f(x)$, with $2 \sin \alpha$, the beam spacing, replacing S. If the spacing of the two beams corresponds to a zero of this radiation pattern, then the two beams are orthogonal.

As an example, consider the case of a uniform distribution over an aperture of length L. The basic radiation pattern is

$$\sin(\pi SL/\lambda)/(\pi SL/\lambda) \tag{6.12}$$

with its first zero when $S = \sin \theta = \lambda/L$, and a first sidelobe level of -13 dB. The squared modulus of a uniform distribution is still a uniform distribution, with the same length L. Its pattern is therefore also given by (6.12). The angular spacing for orthogonal beams corresponds to the zeros of this pattern, which occur when $S = n \lambda/L$ ($n = 1, 2, 3 \ldots$). Figure 6.4 illustrates the above example. The beam 'crossover level' is -4 dB (the field pattern has fallen to $\sin(\pi/2)/(\pi/2) = 2/\pi$ at the crossover point). Because the orthogonality condition is satisfied when $S = n \lambda/L$, a set of orthogonal beams with inter-beam spacing λ/L can be obtained.

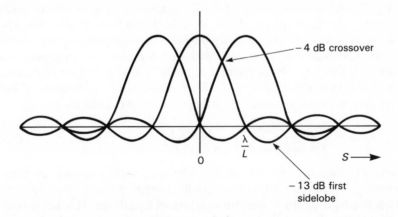

Figure 6.4 Orthogonal 'sin x/x' beams

Figure 6.5 shows four examples of standard aperture distributions (see table 3.1) and their beam orthogonality properties. The basic pattern for $\cos^2(\pi x/L)$ also appears as the 'orthogonality pattern' for $\cos(\pi x/L)$. There are several important properties of orthogonal beams illustrated by these examples. For $f(x) = 1$ (uniform aperture distribution), the orthogonal beam spacings are coincident with the zeros of the basic radiation pattern, $S = n\lambda/L$. The peak of one beam in figure 6.4 is at the same angle as a zero of the other beams. This is not generally true. For the second case in figure 6.5 $f(x) = \cos(\pi x/L)$, the basic pattern zeros are at $S = (n + \frac{1}{2})\lambda/L$, while the orthogonal beam spacings are $S = (n + 1) \lambda/L$, where $n = 1, 2 \ldots$.

The first three examples show an increasing taper, with lower and lower sidelobes in the basic pattern. It is an unfortunate property of orthogonal beams that lower sidelobes generally mean lower beam crossovers; for example, -23 dB sidelobes with -9.5 dB crossovers. This has important implications for multiple beam systems. Very often a system requires low sidelobes and high crossovers, and consequently the multiple beam former has to be lossy (or have significant mutual coupling between beam ports).

Orthogonal beam sets do not always exist for arbitrary aperture distributions. A triangular distribution, example 4 of figure 6.5, does not give any orthogonal beam spacing. The physical explanation is that, since the sidelobes of the basic radiation pattern are all of the same phase, the cross-product of two such patterns cannot average to zero.

Multiple beam formers for linear arrays can take various forms. Three well-established types are illustrated in figure 6.6. These are (a) the Butler matrix (Butler and Lowe, 1961) (b) the Maxon matrix (Hansen, 1966) and (c) the Rotman lens (Rotman and Turner, 1963).

The Butler matrix, figure 6.6(a), consists of a network of hybrid junctions and fixed phase shifts. A hybrid junction divides the power coming in at any one port equally between the two ports on the opposite side of the double line in the inset of figure 6.6(a). In its normal form, using symmetric hybrids, a Butler matrix can only be configured for N elements, where N is an integral power of 2. When connected to an N-element linear array, the network generates N orthogonal beams of the form

$$E(\theta) = \frac{\sin (\pi N d (\sin \theta - \sin \alpha_n)/\lambda)}{\sin (\pi d (\sin \theta - \sin \alpha_n)/\lambda)} \qquad (6.13)$$

where d is the array element spacing. The array excitation for each beam is uniform in amplitude, with phase gradients appropriate to the orthogonal beam positions α_n for a uniform aperture of length Nd. It is important to note that the phase shifts required in the Butler design must be frequency independent. If a Butler matrix is used over a wide bandwidth, the beam-pointing directions will change with frequency (see below) but the crossover point and the orthogonality criterion will hold.

The change of beam direction with frequency is due to the Butler matrix providing a fixed phase gradient from a given beam port. For a linear array with element spacing d, if there is a progressive phase difference of ϕ, the beam is steered to an angle from broadside, where

$$\sin \alpha = -\phi\lambda/(2\pi d) \qquad (6.14)$$

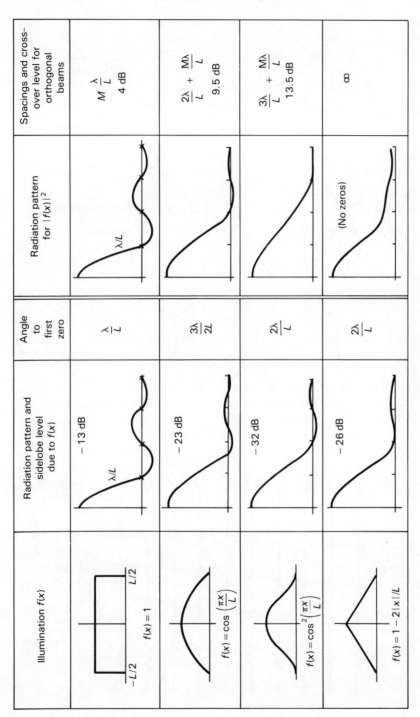

Figure 6.5 Orthogonality properties

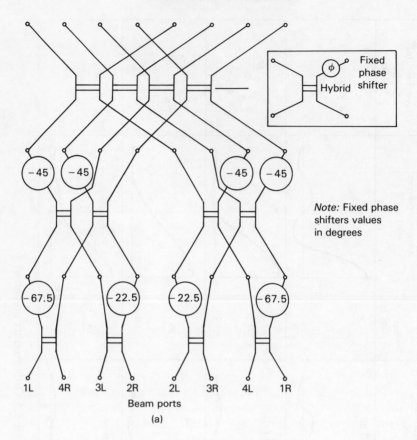

Note: Fixed phase
shifters values
in degrees

(a)

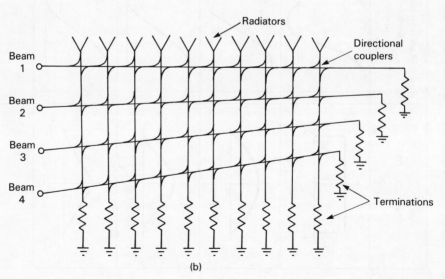

(b)

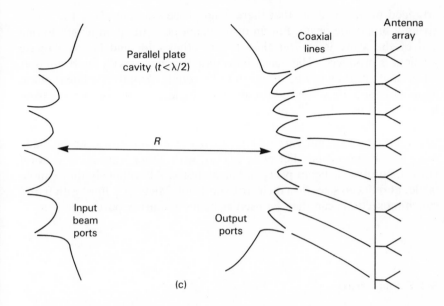

Figure 6.6 (a) Butler matrix. (b) Maxon matrix. (c) Rotman lens

Thus if ϕ and d are fixed, the angle α will vary as λ changes.

The Maxon matrix, figure 6.6(b), is based upon the use of time delays in the antenna feeds to set up the beams from a series of cross-coupling feed-arms. This concept gives far more flexibility of design in terms of amplitude tapers, by varying the coupling values of the directional couplers. The result is not in general an orthogonal system unless this has been built into the design, with consequent loss of flexibility. This matrix can operate over a broad bandwidth, and as the frequency changes the beam-pointing directions will not change (see below), but the crossover points will. Orthogonality is not maintained over a band.

The Maxon matrix is a time delay (path length), rather than phase shift, device. This means that, as the frequency changes, the phase differences also change, in direct proportion to the frequency. As the wavelength λ varies inversely with the frequency, the product $\phi\lambda$ in (6.14) remains constant, so the beam angle α does not vary with frequency.

Figure 6.6(c) shows a Rotman lens multiple beam former. This contains a parallel plate region, with plate separation less than $\lambda/2$, so that only a TEM mode can propagate. Beam ports and array ports are arranged along prescribed contours, and r.f. cables of specified (unequal) lengths connect the array ports to the array elements. The lens contours and the cable lengths are design variables which are used to optimise the scanning performance. For the central beam port, the total path lengths across the parallel plate region and through the cables to the array elements are arranged to be equal, so that there is no phase gradient along the array, giving a broadside beam. For an offset beam port, the path length to one end of the array is shorter than to the other end, and hence a phase gradient is produced. The beam deflection ψ increases with the beam port offset angle θ (they can be designed to be equal). A perfectly linear phase gradient cannot be produced for all beam angles, but the departures from linearity can usually be kept small.

Because the Rotman lens design is based on path length differences, the beam directions do not vary with frequency. Rotman lenses can be made using an air-spaced parallel plate region, with either waveguide sectoral horns or probes as beam ports and array ports. Alternatively they can be made, at reduced size, on a dielectric substrate. Microstrip lines with flared matching sections can then be used as beam and array ports.

6.4 Planar arrays

Just as a linear array can be considered as a sampled aperture in two dimensions, a planar array can be thought of as a sampled aperture in three dimensions. The analysis in section 3.4 of planar apertures is therefore appropriate to derive many of the properties of planar arrays, provided they are at least several wavelengths across and are composed of elements which radiate predominantly into one half-space, such as open-ended waveguides, or dipoles in front of a planar reflecting sheet. Typical aperture shapes are rectangular, elliptical or circular. Figure 6.7 shows two standard array 'lattices': (a) a rectangular grid and (b) a triangular grid.

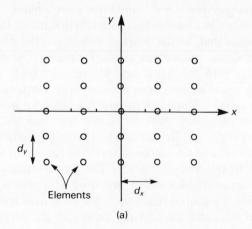

(a)

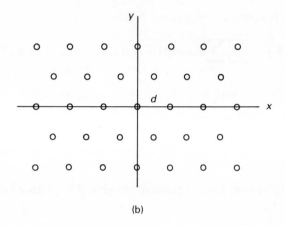

(b)

Figure 6.7 (a) Rectangular lattice. (b) Triangular lattice

Beamwidths and first sidelobe levels can generally be found using continuous aperture theory (section 3.4). The 'far out' sidelobe levels need array calculations. Beam steering to a direction (S_{10}, S_{20}) can be accomplished using the appropriate phase distribution. The direction cosines S_1 and S_2 are

$$S_1 = \sin \theta \cos \phi, \quad S_2 = \sin \theta \sin \phi \tag{6.15}$$

where θ and ϕ are the usual spherical polar coordinates with respect to z as the normal to the array aperture. Let the element lattice spacings in the x and y directions be d_x and d_y (for either type of lattice in figure 6.7). Then the inter-element phase shifts in the x and y directions need to be

$$\phi_x = -k \, d_x \, S_{10}, \quad \phi_y = -k \, d_y \, S_{20} \tag{6.16}$$

in order to steer the beam to (θ_0, ϕ_0).

As the beam is scanned, its beamwidth changes as the inverse of the projected aperture. For a rectangular aperture, with an aperture distribution separable in x and y, and scanned in one of the two principal planes (x–z or y–z), the beamwidth varies approximately as $1/\cos \alpha$, as described at the end of section 3.3. For scanning in intermediate planes, or for other aperture shapes, the calculation is more complicated.

In chapter 4, the conditions for the appearance of grating lobes were analysed for a linear array. For a planar array, there are different results for a rectangular lattice and a triangular lattice (see figure 6.7). Consider a rectangular lattice with inter-element spacings d_x and d_y. The array factor for an unsteered beam is

$$P(S_1, S_2) = \sum_l \sum_m a_{lm} \exp\{jk \, (l \, d_x \, S_1 + m \, d_y \, S_2)\} \tag{6.17}$$

If the beam is now steered to (S_{10}, S_{20}):

$$P(S_1, S_2) = \sum\sum a_{lm} \exp\{jk\ (l\ d_x(S_1 - S_{10}) + m\ d_y(S_2 - S_{20})\}$$

(6.18)

The main lobe is where $S_1 = S_{10}$, $S_2 = S_{20}$. A grating lobe will appear if

$$k\ d_x(S_1 - S_{10}) = 2\pi n$$

or   (6.19)

$$k\ d_y(S_2 - S_{20}) = 2\pi p$$

where n and p are negative or positive integers. The grating lobe conditions
are thus:

$$S_1 - S_{10} = \frac{\lambda}{d_x} \cdot n$$

or   (6.20)

$$S_2 - S_{20} = \frac{\lambda}{d_y} \cdot p$$

A rectangular lattice scanned in a principal plane behaves similarly to a
linear array. For arbitrary scan angles, the diagram shown as figure
6.8(a) can be used. This shows the 'inverse lattice' for the rectangular grid
array, with lattice points spaced by λ/d_x and λ/d_y. The inverse lattice
coordinates are $S_1 - S_{10}$ and $S_2 - S_{20}$. The inverse lattice points correspond to the main beam and grating lobes.

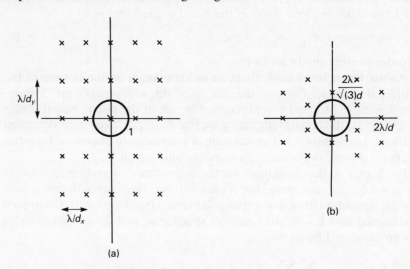

(a)

Figure 6.8 (a) Inverse lattice for a rectangular grid. (b) Inverse lattice for an
     equilateral triangle grid

For a broadside beam, $S_{10} = S_{20} = 0$, and the coordinates become S_1, S_2. For arbitrary observation angles θ, ϕ, $S_1^2 + S_2^2 < 1$, and a circle of unit radius encompasses all possible cases. If this circle does not include any inverse lattice points (other than 0,0), grating lobes will not appear. Then the condition for no grating lobes becomes

$$d_x < \lambda \text{ and } d_y < \lambda \tag{6.21}$$

for an unsteered beam.

Now let the main beam be scanned to a direction (S_{10}, S_{20}). The unit circle is centred where $S_1 = 0$, $S_2 = 0$, which is now at coordinates $(-S_{10}, -S_{20})$ in figure 6.8(a). If the circle now includes inverse lattice points other than $(0,0)$, grating lobes will occur. If the scan angle from broadside is θ_0, the centre of the circle is displaced from $(0,0)$ by a radial distance $\sin \theta_0 \; (= \sqrt{(S_{10}^2 + S_{20}^2)})$. Now if the beam can be steered anywhere within a cone about broadside with maximum scan angle θ_0, a circle centred at $(0,0)$ with radius $1 + \sin \theta_0$ encompasses all the possible cases. The condition for no grating lobes is then

$$d_x < \lambda/(1 + \sin \theta_0) \text{ and } d_y < \lambda/(1 + \sin \theta_0) \tag{6.22}$$

Now consider a special case of figure 6.7(b), where the triangles are made equilateral, with nearest neighbour spacing d. This has the inverse lattice shown in figure 6.8(b). The 'x' spacing in the inverse lattice is $2\lambda/d$, because the *lines* of elements are $d/2$ apart in the x direction. Similarly, the 'y' spacing is $2\lambda/\sqrt{(3)}d$, because the lines of elements are spaced by $\sqrt{(3)}d/2$ in the y direction. The other points in the inverse lattice follow from symmetry considerations. For the unscanned case, $S_{10} = S_{20} = 0$, a circle of unit radius is used, and the condition for no grating lobes is

$$d < 2\lambda/\sqrt{3} \tag{6.23}$$

For scanning within a cone of semi-angle θ_0, the condition becomes

$$d < 2\lambda/[\sqrt{(3)}\{1 + \sin \theta_0\}] \tag{6.24}$$

A square lattice with spacing d has an area per element, A_{el}, of d^2, whereas an equilateral triangle lattice with spacing d has an area per element of $[\sqrt{(3)}/2]d^2$. If we consider the conditions for no grating lobes, without scanning in the two cases:

$$A_{el} \begin{pmatrix} \text{square} \\ \text{lattice} \end{pmatrix} < \lambda^2$$

$$A_{el} \begin{pmatrix} \text{triangular} \\ \text{lattice} \end{pmatrix} < [\sqrt{(3)}/2] \, [2/\sqrt{(3)}]^2 \, \lambda^2 = [2/\sqrt{(3)}] \, \lambda^2 \tag{6.25}$$

For scanning out to θ_0, both areas are reduced by the same factor $(1 + \sin \theta_0)^2$. The equilateral triangular lattice thus allows a greater area per element than a square lattice, for grating lobe free performance. Fewer array elements, 86.6 per cent, can then be used.

A planar array can be fed in various ways. Figure 6.9 shows a corporate (parallel) amplitude distribution network for a planar array. This could be used with phase shifters at each element to provide a steerable single beam. This approach has several drawbacks, notably the high cost of phase shifters, and an interconnection problem. As well as connections to the array elements, the phase shifters need control lines, and a thin planar structure for the complete antenna assembly is difficult to achieve.

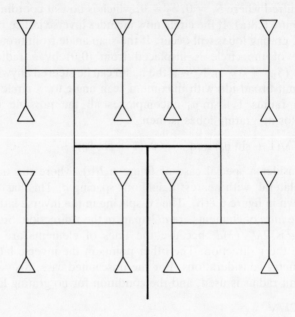

Figure 6.9 Corporate (parallel) feed for a planar array

A planar array is often fed with separable 'beam forming' in two orthogonal planes. Here 'beam forming' means either providing the amplitude and phase distribution required for a single beam, or forming simultaneous multiple beams. As an example, phase shift scanning in one plane can be combined with frequency scanning in the other. The corporate feed and phase shifters are then similar to those for a linear array of n elements, for a planar array with $N = n \times m$ elements. There would then be n series-fed arrays of m elements.

A second example is an array where each row has a fixed corporate feed, and the rows are combined using a simultaneous multiple beam former. Such an array can be scanned by mechanical rotation in azimuth, while covering a wide elevation sector with simultaneous high gain beams.

6.5 Mutual coupling in phased arrays

In the analysis of linear and planar arrays, it has been indicated that the radiation pattern of the array is the product of the array factor and the element pattern. Two caveats are needed. Firstly, the element pattern is not in general that of the element in isolation, due to the effects of its neighbours. If one element is fed, its neighbours are excited due to mutual coupling, hence giving a different radiation pattern to that of the element in isolation. Secondly, there are 'edge' effects, particularly in a small array, because elements near the edges of the array do not see the same distribution of neighbours as near the centre, and therefore the effects of mutual coupling differ.

If we ignore edge effects, the array radiation pattern can be written as the product of the array factor and the 'active element pattern'. The active element pattern can be measured with that element excited and all other elements present and terminated in matched loads. Let the array factor be $N h (S_1, S_2)$, where the peak value of h is unity (and N is the number of elements). The array gain pattern is then:

$$G(S_1, S_2) = Ng_a(S_1, S_2)h^2 (S_1, S_2) \qquad (6.26)$$

where g_a is the active element gain pattern.

Active element patterns can exhibit several notable features, (i) flattening of the 'beam' peak, and (ii) deep dips in the pattern. Neither of these effects are present in the isolated element pattern.

Consider what happens when the whole array is excited, with the main beam scanned to the angle of a deep dip. The elements will be unable to radiate any significant fraction of the available power. There must therefore be a severe mismatch, resulting in most of the incident power being reflected. Such a scan direction is called a 'blind spot'. Clearly it is important to design a phased array such that blind spots only occur outside the desired range of scan angles.

Mutual coupling analysis is complicated; either an element-by-element approach, or a receive analysis using the periodic properties of an infinite array, may be used for certain standard configurations. Amitay *et al*. (1972), Stark (1974) and Rudge *et al*. (1982) give detailed analyses. Experimental measurement of active element patterns may be required. How significant the effects are depends on the type of element, the array lattice type, the array spacings and which pattern cut/plane of scan is being considered.

Provided that blind spots, if they occur, are outside the required range of scan angles, array analysis ignoring mutual coupling can make reasonable predictions. The array factor tends to dominate the radiation pattern and gain, so that the precise pattern of the element becomes less important. Clearly there are potential problems for wide angle scanning, or for very low sidelobe systems where precise predictions are needed. Feed network design may have to cope with significant mismatch reflections.

6.6 Circular arrays

Antenna arrays do not have to be linear or planar; curved arcs or surfaces
can also be used. 'Conformal' arrays follow a defined surface such as the
fuselage of an aircraft. Their analysis and feed design are usually more
complex, making synthesis of a desired pattern more difficult. One
relatively well studied case is that of a complete circular or ring array
(Rudge *et al.*, 1982b).

The first thing to note about circular arrays is that the idea of an array
factor multiplying an element pattern is not generally applicable. The
elements usually point outwards along a radius, so that the array has
circular symmetry.

One possible excitation of a circular array to form a beam is to feed all
elements with the same amplitudes, and to arrange their phases such that
they give co-phased contributions for a particular direction. Figure 6.10

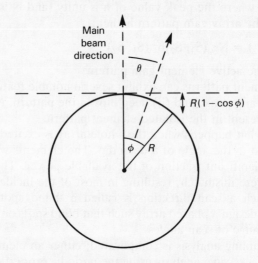

Figure 6.10 Circular array geometry

shows the geometry. The required phase for an array element placed at an
angle ϕ_n around the circle is

$$\alpha_n = (2\pi R/\lambda)\,(1 - \cos\phi_n) \tag{6.27}$$

The radiation pattern for omnidirectional elements (that is, isotropic in
the plane of the circle) in the array plane is

$$E(\theta) = \sum_{n=1}^{N} \exp\{j\alpha_n\} \cdot \exp\left\{-j\frac{2\pi R}{\lambda}(1 - \cos(\phi - \theta))\right\}$$

$$= \sum_{n=1}^{N} \exp\left\{-j\frac{2\pi R}{\lambda}[\cos(\phi - \theta) - \cos\phi]\right\} \tag{6.28}$$

For large numbers of elements and close element spacings, this summation can be approximated by an integral. The pattern then becomes

$$E(\theta) = J_0\left\{\frac{4\pi R}{\lambda}\sin(\theta/2)\right\} \tag{6.29}$$

where J_0 is a Bessel function. The first sidelobe of this pattern is -9 dB relative to the main beam. This is because the projection of an equispaced circular array onto a linear aperture has an increased concentration of elements at the edges — that is, an 'inverse taper'.

Low sidelobes can be achieved if the amplitude distribution has a symmetrical taper on the 'front' half of the array, with very low or zero excitation on the other half.

Beam steering from an arc array can be achieved by varying the element phase distribution, similar in principle to a linear array. An alternative beam-steering technique is to shift the amplitude and phase excitation around the arc or circle, keeping the beam in a radial direction. This requires electronic control of both amplitude and phase. Multiple beams from a circular or arc array can be obtained using a circular lens (Archer, 1975). There are various types, some using phase steering and some shifting the excitation around the array.

A rather different approach to the excitation of complete circular arrays involves the use of 'phase modes' (Rudge *et al.*, 1982b). The circular array is approximated as a continuous ring source. Then if the array excitation has a constant amplitude plus an integral (m) cycles of phase variation round the circumference, the resulting far field pattern also has a constant amplitude and a similar variation of phase with angle. Thus if the excitation is

$$I = A\exp(jm\phi) \tag{6.30}$$

the pattern is

$$E(\theta) = A \cdot j^m \cdot J_m(2\pi R/\lambda)\exp(jm\theta) \tag{6.31}$$

where the J_m are Bessel functions.

Because the array excitation is periodic in angle with period 2π radians, it can always be expressed as a complex Fourier series where the (spatial) harmonics are the phase modes. Then the array excitation $I(\phi)$ can be expressed as

$$I(\phi) = \sum I_m \exp(jm\phi) \tag{6.32}$$

and the overall radiation pattern can be found using (6.31).

As an example, if $2N+1$ phase modes are excited with

$$I_m = \frac{1}{j^m \cdot J_m(2\pi R/\lambda)} \tag{6.33}$$

$$E(\theta) = \sum_{-N}^{N} \exp(jm\theta) = \frac{\sin N\theta}{\sin \theta} \tag{6.34}$$

this pattern has the usual -13 dB sidelobes, but uses a θ (rather than $\sin \theta$) scale.

The number of phase modes which can be excited depends on the number of discrete elements in the array. At least $2N$ elements are needed for phase modes for $-N$ to $+N$. For a good approximation to the continuous aperture mode patterns, the array spacing d needs to be $\leqslant \lambda/2$. If $d = \lambda/2$, the zero-to-zero beamwidth of the pattern (6.34) is

$$\Delta\theta = 2\lambda/D \tag{6.35}$$

where D is the array diameter. A linear array of length equal to the array diameter has $\Delta (\sin \theta) = 2\lambda/D$.

In order to excite such a set of phase modes, the most convenient scheme is to use a Butler matrix as shown in figure 6.11. In this case each array port

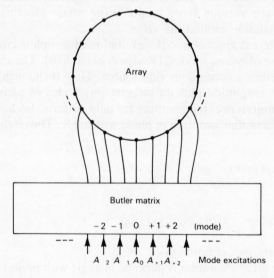

Figure 6.11 Butler matrix for phase mode excitation

of the matrix is fed to an element of the circular array and each beam port corresponds to a feed port which excites a different phase mode. For example, an 8×8 Butler matrix can be used with an 8-element circular array to give modes $-3, -2 \ldots +4$ (the -4 mode is identical to the $+4$) mode).

A further property of the phase modes is that the application of a linear progressive phase shift $0, \alpha, 2\alpha, 3\alpha \ldots$ to the mode ports causes the radiation pattern to be rotated in azimuth by an angle α. For example, equation (6.34) then becomes

$$E(\theta) = \sum_{-N}^{N} \exp\{jm(\theta + \alpha)\} = \frac{\sin(N(\theta + \alpha))}{\sin(\theta + \alpha)} \tag{6.36}$$

6.7 Case study: a Rotman lens multiple beam former

A Rotman lens is a multiple beam-forming device which was described briefly in section 6.3. A more detailed look at a Rotman lens illustrates several aspects of the theory given in this chapter and those preceding.

Figure 6.12(a) shows the parameters of a Rotman lens-fed linear array. The array elements have specified positions y_3 (coordinates normalised to the lens length are used to generate 'universal' designs). Lengths w of transmission line (for example, coaxial cable) connect the array elements to 'array ports' with coordinates (x_2, y_2). The locus $x_2 (y_2)$ is called the 'array port contour'. On the other side of the parallel plate region there are several 'beam ports' with coordinates (x_1, y_1). The 'beam port contour' is the locus $x_1 (y_1)$. The Rotman lens consists of all this structure except for the array itself. An analogous optical lens would consist of the array port contour, the transmission lines and the array, with the centre of the beam port contour as the lens focus.

How is this 'microwave lens' actually constructed? The parallel plate region can consist of two metal plates spaced by less than $\lambda/2$. This forces the electric field to be normal to the plates, the magnetic field to be parallel to them, and thus only a TEM mode with velocity c can propagate. (This assumes the region is many wavelengths across.) The region is then essentially a two-dimensional 'free space'. The lens ports can be either (flared) open-ended waveguides (Smith and Fong, 1983) or monopole-like probes with a reflecting strip about $\lambda/4$ behind, so that the reflected signal adds to the probe's forward radiation (Rotman and Turner, 1963). Another method of construction is to use a printed microstrip design. Figure 6.12(b) shows a microstrip Rotman lens (Fong and Smith, 1984). The flared microstrip transitions act rather like waveguide ports; the thin microstrip lines are equivalent to coaxial cables.

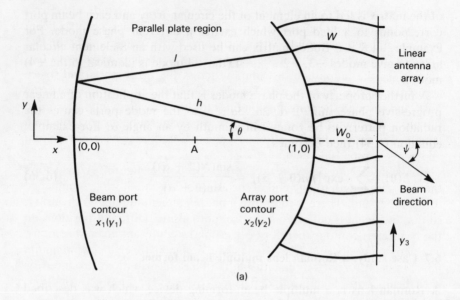

(a)

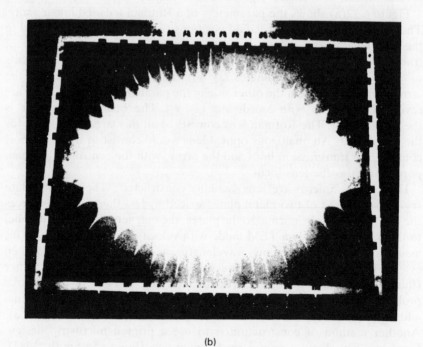

(b)

Figure 6.12 (a) Normalised geometry of a Rotman lens. (b) Microstrip Rotman lens

In order to form a beam from a linear array, an amplitude and phase distribution needs to be created across the array. Consider a central beam port, say a flared waveguide with aperture width *l*. Aperture theory in two dimensions (section 3.2) can be used to find its radiation pattern. This determines the amplitude distribution across the array ports and hence across the array. The total path lengths from the beam port to each array port, and through the transmission lines to the array elements, determine the phase distribution along the array. For the central beam port, the path lengths are arranged to be all equal, giving a uniform phase distribution and hence a broadside beam.

Now consider an offset beam port. Inspection of figure 6.12(a) shows that the path length to one end of the array is shortened, while lengthened to the other end. There is therefore a phase gradient applied to the array, so that the beam is deflected away from broadside. Different positions on the beam port contour therefore correspond to different beam directions. The lens contours and line lengths are designed to give the minimum possible departures from linearity in the phase distributions produced by each beam port. Significant departures from linear phase distributions distort the beam shape and raise sidelobe levels.

Figure 6.13 shows some measured multiple beam radiation patterns at 10 GHz for a waveguide-fed Rotman lens connected to a sixteen-element array of monopoles with a plane reflector $\lambda/4$ behind. It is noteworthy that the multiple beam set is quite a good approximation to the orthogonal beam set appropriate to a half-cosine aperture distribution (figure 6.5). This has sidelobes of -23 dB and beam crossovers of -9.5 dB. The explanation for this is as follows. The number of beams within the scan sector is determined by how many flared waveguide beam ports can fit along the beam port contour. The width of the beam port apertures was chosen so that the main beam of the beam port's radiation pattern just covers the array ports. Then little power is lost by 'spillover' within the lens, and a tapered amplitude distribution (fairly similar to a half-cosine) is set up over the array aperture. Mutual coupling between flared waveguides side by side is fairly low, so the conditions for orthogonal beams are approximately met. Given the array aperture distribution, the multiple beam set of figure 6.13 is therefore consistent with our expectations.

Non-orthogonal multiple beam sets can be obtained with the addition of beam overlap networks (White, 1962; Smith, 1985), which trade off some loss against higher beam crossover levels.

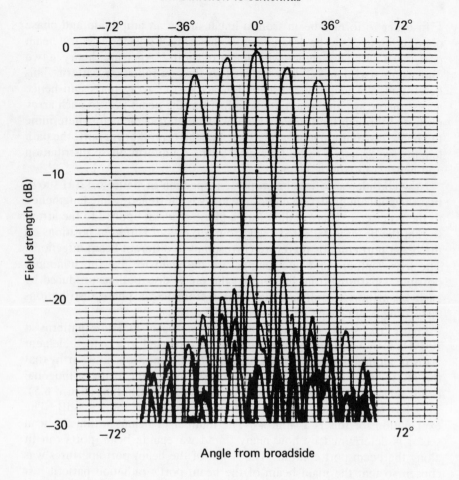

Figure 6.13 Measured multiple beam radiation patterns of a lens-fed array

References

Amitay, N., Galindo, V. and Wu, C. P. (1972). *Theory and Analysis of Phased Array Antennas*, Wiley, New York.

Archer, D. (1975). 'Lens fed multiple beam arrays', *Microwave J.*, *18*, pp.37–42.

Butler, J. and Lowe, R. (1961). 'Beamforming matrix simplifies design of electronically scanned antennas', *Electronics Design*, *9*, p.170.

Fong, A. K. S. and Smith, M. S. (1984). 'A microstrip multiple beam forming lens', *Radio and Electronic Engineer*, *54*, pp.318–20.

Hansen, R. (Ed.) (1966). *Microwave Scanning Antennas, Vol. III*, Academic Press, London, chapter 3.

Rotman, W. and Turner, R. F. (1963). 'Wide angle lens for line source applications', *IEEE Trans.*, *AP-11*, pp.623–32.

Rudge, A. W., Milne, K., Olver, A. D. and Knight, P. (Eds) (1982). *The Handbook of Antenna Design*, Peter Peregrinus, Hitchin, Herts, (a) chapter 10, (b) chapter 12.

Smith, M. S. (1985). 'Multiple beam crossovers for a lens fed antenna array', *J.I.E.R.E.*, *55*, pp.33–6.

Smith, M. S. and Fong, A. K. S. (1983). 'Amplitude performance of Ruze and Rotman lenses', *Radio and Electronic Engineer*, *53*, pp.329–36.

Stark, L. (1974). 'Microwave theory of phased array antennas — a review', *Proc. IEEE*, *62*, pp.1661–701.

White, W. D. (1962). 'Pattern limitations in multiple beam antennas', *IRE Trans.*, *AP-10*, pp.430–6.

Appendix A: Vector Differential Operators

Divergence ($\nabla \cdot$)

Cartesian

$$\nabla \cdot \boldsymbol{D} = \frac{\partial D_x}{\partial x} + \frac{\partial D_y}{\partial y} + \frac{\partial D_z}{\partial z}$$

Cylindrical

$$\nabla \cdot \boldsymbol{D} = \frac{1}{r} \frac{\partial}{\partial r} (r D_r) + \frac{1}{r} \frac{\partial D_\phi}{\partial \phi} + \frac{\partial D_z}{\partial z}$$

Spherical

$$\nabla \cdot \boldsymbol{D} = \frac{1}{r^2} \frac{\partial}{\partial r} (r^2 D_r) + \frac{1}{r \sin \theta} \frac{\partial}{\partial \theta} (\sin \theta \, D_\theta) + \frac{1}{r \sin \theta} \frac{\partial D_\phi}{\partial \phi}$$

Gradient (∇)

Cartesian

$$\nabla V = \frac{\partial V}{\partial x} \boldsymbol{u}_x + \frac{\partial V}{\partial y} \boldsymbol{u}_y + \frac{\partial V}{\partial z} \boldsymbol{u}_z$$

Cylindrical

$$\nabla V = \frac{\partial V}{\partial r} \boldsymbol{u}_r + \frac{1}{r} \frac{\partial V}{\partial \phi} \boldsymbol{u}_\phi + \frac{\partial V}{\partial z} \boldsymbol{u}_z$$

Spherical

$$\nabla V = \frac{\partial V}{\partial r} \boldsymbol{u}_r + \frac{1}{r} \frac{\partial V}{\partial \theta} \boldsymbol{u}_\theta + \frac{1}{r \sin \theta} \frac{\partial V}{\partial \phi} \boldsymbol{u}_\phi$$

Curl ($\nabla \times$)

Cartesian

$$\nabla \times \boldsymbol{H} = \left(\frac{\partial H_z}{\partial y} - \frac{\partial H_y}{\partial z}\right) \boldsymbol{u}_x + \left(\frac{\partial H_x}{\partial z} - \frac{\partial H_z}{\partial x}\right) \boldsymbol{u}_y + \left(\frac{\partial H_y}{\partial x} - \frac{\partial H_z}{\partial y}\right) \boldsymbol{u}_z$$

Cylindrical

$$\nabla \times \boldsymbol{H} = \left(\frac{1}{r}\frac{\partial H_z}{\partial \phi} - \frac{\partial H_\phi}{\partial z}\right) \boldsymbol{u}_r + \left(\frac{\partial H_r}{\partial z} - \frac{\partial H_z}{\partial r}\right) \boldsymbol{u}_\phi + \frac{1}{r}\left[\frac{\partial (rH_\phi)}{\partial r} - \frac{\partial H_r}{\partial \phi}\right] \boldsymbol{u}_z$$

Spherical

$$\nabla \times \boldsymbol{H} = \frac{1}{r \sin \theta}\left[\frac{\partial (H_\phi \sin \theta)}{\partial \theta} - \frac{\partial H_\theta}{\partial \phi}\right] \boldsymbol{u}_r + \frac{1}{r}\left[\frac{1}{\sin \theta}\frac{\partial H_r}{\partial \phi} - \frac{\partial (rH_\phi)}{\partial r}\right] \boldsymbol{u}_\theta$$

$$+ \frac{1}{r}\left[\frac{\partial (rH_\theta)}{\partial r} - \frac{\partial H_r}{\partial \theta}\right] \boldsymbol{u}_\phi$$

Laplacian (∇^2)

Cartesian

$$\nabla^2 V = \frac{\partial^2 V}{\partial x^2} + \frac{\partial^2 V}{\partial y^2} + \frac{\partial^2 V}{\partial z^2}$$

Cylindrical

$$\nabla^2 V = \frac{1}{r}\frac{\partial}{\partial r}\left(r\frac{\partial V}{\partial r}\right) + \frac{1}{r^2}\frac{\partial^2 V}{\partial \phi^2} + \frac{\partial^2 V}{\partial z^2}$$

Spherical

$$\nabla^2 V = \frac{1}{r^2}\frac{\partial}{\partial r}\left(r^2\frac{\partial V}{\partial r}\right) + \frac{1}{r^2 \sin \theta}\frac{\partial}{\partial \theta}\left(\sin \theta \frac{\partial V}{\partial \theta}\right) + \frac{1}{r^2 \sin^2 \theta}\frac{\partial^2 V}{\partial \phi^2}$$

Appendix B: The Fields of a Hertzian Dipole

In section 2.2, it was shown that the magnetic vector potential A of a current element $I\,dl$ (z-directed) is

$$A_z = \frac{I\,dl}{4\pi} \cdot \frac{\exp(-jkr)}{r} \tag{B.1}$$

To find E and H, we use

$$H = \text{curl}\,A \tag{B.2}$$

$$E = \frac{1}{j\omega\epsilon_0}\,\text{curl}\,H \tag{B.3}$$

which are respectively (2.4) and (2.2) with $J = 0$ (outside the source region). Then

$$H = \text{curl}\,(A_z\,\boldsymbol{u}_z) = (\text{grad}\,A_z) \times \boldsymbol{u}_z\,(+\,A_z\,\text{curl}\,\boldsymbol{u}_z = 0) \tag{B.4}$$

Because A_z is a function of r only:

$$\text{grad}\,A_z = \frac{\partial A_z}{\partial r} \cdot \boldsymbol{u}_r$$

$$H = \frac{I\,dl}{4\pi} \left\{ \frac{-jk\,\exp(-jkr)}{r} - \frac{\exp(-jkr)}{r^2} \right\} \boldsymbol{u}_r \times \boldsymbol{u}_z \tag{B.5}$$

$$= \frac{I\,dl}{4\pi} \left\{ \frac{jk}{r} + \frac{1}{r^2} \right\} \cdot \exp(-jkr) \cdot \sin\theta \cdot \boldsymbol{u}_\phi \tag{B.6}$$

Then the electric field becomes

$$E = \frac{1}{j\omega\epsilon_0}\,\text{curl}(H_\phi)$$

$$= \frac{1}{j\omega\epsilon_0} \left\{ \boldsymbol{u}_r \cdot \frac{1}{r\sin\theta} \frac{\partial(H_\phi\,\sin\theta)}{\partial\theta} - \boldsymbol{u}_\theta \cdot \frac{1}{r} \frac{\partial(r\,H_\phi)}{\partial r} \right\} \tag{B.7}$$

Then

$$E_r = \frac{I \, dl}{j\omega 4\pi\epsilon_0} \cdot \frac{1}{r \sin \theta} \left(\frac{jk}{r} + \frac{1}{r^2} \right) \exp(-jkr) \frac{\partial}{\partial\theta} (\sin^2\theta)$$

$$= \frac{I \, dl}{2\pi} \cdot jk \, Z_0 \left\{ \frac{1}{jkr} + \frac{1}{(jkr)^2} \right\} \frac{\exp(-jkr)}{r} \cdot \cos \theta \qquad \text{(B.8)}$$

$$E_\theta = \frac{I \, dl}{j\omega 4\pi\epsilon_0} \cdot \frac{-1}{r} \cdot \sin \theta \cdot \frac{\partial}{\partial r} \left\{ \left(jk + \frac{1}{r} \right) \exp(-jkr) \right\}$$

$$= \frac{I \, dl}{4\pi} \cdot jk \, Z_0 \left\{ 1 + \frac{1}{jkr} + \frac{1}{(jkr)^2} \right\} \frac{\exp(-jkr)}{r} \sin \theta \qquad \text{(B.9)}$$

Appendix C: Derivation of Aperture Theory in Three Dimensions

Suppose that the electric field is linearly polarised in the aperture plane $z = 0$ and E is parallel to the x axis. Then we can write

$$E_x(x, y, 0) = \int_{-\infty}^{\infty} \int_{-\infty}^{\infty} P(S_1, S_2) \exp(-jkS_1x - jkS_2y) \, dS_1 \, dS_2 \qquad (C.1)$$

(*Note*: Other Fourier transform conventions are possible, with different numerical factors.) Here $P(S_1, S_2)$ is the Fourier transform of $E_x(x, y, 0)$, the aperture plane electric field. The inverse relation is

$$P(S_1, S_2) = \frac{1}{(2\pi)^2} \iint E_x(x, y, 0) \exp\{jkS_1x + jkS_2y\} \, d(kx) \, d(ky) \qquad (C.2)$$

Now any plane wave travelling in a direction θ, ϕ has

$$E_x(x, y, z) = E \exp[-jk(x \sin \theta \cos \phi + y \sin \theta \sin \phi + z \cos \theta)] \qquad (C.3)$$

When $z = 0$, the variation with x and y is of the same form as in (C.1) above, provided that

$$S_1 = \sin \theta \cos \phi \quad \text{and} \quad S_2 = \sin \theta \sin\phi \qquad (C.4)$$

We can therefore regard equation (C.1) as stating that the aperture field arises from a collection of plane waves travelling in all possible directions, the amplitude of the wave in the direction given by S_1, S_2 being $P(S_1, S_2)$. Each of these waves varies with z in a manner specified by (C.3), so that we find the radiated field to be

$$E_x(x, y, z) = \iint P(S_1, S_2) \exp\{-jk(S_1x + S_2y + Cz)\} \, dS_1 dS_2 \qquad (C.5)$$

where

$$C = (1 - S_1^2 - S_2^2)^{1/2} \qquad (C.6)$$

When θ and ϕ are real angles, C is real and the positive square root in (C.6) is used. The Fourier representation, however, requires that S_1 and S_2 can assume any real values, so that C can become imaginary; the root is then selected to make C a negative imaginary quantity, making the field decay exponentially with increasing positive values of z (a three-dimensional case of the inhomogeneous plane wave).

Expressions for the other field components can be derived by considering equations corresponding to (C.3). In vector form these are

$$E(x, y, z) = \iint (Cu_x - S_1 \, u_z) \, P(S_1, S_2) \exp[-jk(S_1 x + S_2 y + Cz)] \, \mathrm{d}S_1 \, \mathrm{d}S_2/C \quad (C.7)$$

$$H(x, y, z) = \frac{1}{Z_0} \iint [-S_1 \, S_2 u_x + (1 - S_2^2)u_y - CS_2 u_z] \, P(S_1, S_2) \times \quad (C.8)$$

$$\exp[-jk(S_1 x + S_2 y + Cz)] \, \mathrm{d}S_1 \, \mathrm{d}S_2/C$$

(Here u_x, u_y, u_z are unit vectors in the x, y and z directions.)

When the aperture field has no y component of electric field, this component vanishes everywhere. Corresponding results can be derived when $E_x = 0$, and the most general case can always be resolved into a sum of the two linearly polarised cases.

The field at a point sufficiently distant from the aperture plane can be calculated approximately by a double application of the stationary phase method to (C.7) and (C.8) (as in the two-dimensional case). In spherical polar coordinates (r, θ, ϕ)

$$E(r, \theta, \phi) = \frac{\lambda}{r} \cdot \exp\{-j(kr - \pi/2)\} \times (\cos \phi \; \hat{u}_\theta - \sin \phi \cos \theta \; \hat{u}_\phi)$$

$$\times \begin{cases} P(\sin \theta \cos \phi, \sin \theta \sin \phi) \\ P(S_1, S_2) \end{cases} \quad (C.9)$$

$$H(r, \theta, \phi) = \frac{1}{Z_0} \times \hat{u}_r \times E(r, \theta, \phi) \quad (C.10)$$

Compare with the two-dimensional result:

$$E_\theta(r, \theta) = P(\sin \theta) \sqrt{\left(\frac{\lambda}{r}\right)} \exp(-j(kr - \pi/4))$$

The dominant variation of the far field with direction is due to $P(S_1, S_2)$, which can therefore be interpreted as the *amplitude radiation pattern*. The requirement on r for the approximation to be reasonable is that it is large compared with the wavelength and with the dimensions of the aperture plane over which there is appreciable illumination.

Equation (C.9) is similar to the result obtained by using the Huyghens–Kirchhoff integral method in the Fraunhofer region. The results often quoted give

$$E(r, \theta, \phi) = j\frac{(1 + \cos \theta) \cdot \exp(-jkr)}{2\lambda r} \times (\cos \phi \hat{u}_\theta - \sin \phi \hat{u}_\phi) \times P(S_1, S_2)$$

(C.11)

(*Note*: Now
$$P(S_1,S_2) = 1 \cdot \int E_x \ldots \, dx \, dy \quad \text{and} \quad E_x = \frac{1}{\lambda^2} \iint \ldots \, dS_1 \, dS_2.)$$

This *differs* from (C.9) only in the angular factors multiplying P. For small values of θ the expressions are virtually identical ($\cos \theta \approx 1$).

The two solutions differ despite being apparently based on identical approximations, namely $kr \gg 1$. The most significant difference is that (C.9) only requires a knowledge of E_x in the aperture plane, while the Kirchhoff method requires both E and H to be specified. These fields are not necessarily *consistent*. The result (C.11) uses the *assumption* that E and H are related as in a plane wave, which is never exactly true for a finite aperture.

However, $E_x(x, y, 0)$ is not known exactly either, and assumptions about it are usually made. The same E_x assumptions will give slightly different (C.9) and (C.11). (We can derive (C.11) as $\frac{1}{2} \times E_x$ solution $+ \frac{1}{2} \times H_y$ solution.)

Exercises

Chapter 2

2.1 Deduce (2.18) from (2.15) and (2.17).

2.2 Complete the algebraic derivation of (2.24).

2.3 Calculate the gain of a Hertzian dipole, assuming it is 100 per cent efficient, by integrating the radiated power and comparing peak to average.

2.4 Derive (2.30) using the far fields of a small, square loop.

2.5 Complete the derivation of (2.31).

Chapter 3

3.1 Calculate the radiation pattern corresponding to the aperture distribution

$$E_x(x, 0) = \begin{cases} \exp(-x/a), & x \geq 0 \\ 0, & x < 0 \end{cases}$$

3.2 Complete the algebraic derivation of (3.45).

3.3 It is required to produce a radiation pattern in which the amplitude varies as a half-cosine wave between the limits $\pm \sin \theta$ on a $\sin \alpha$ scale, and is zero outside these limits. What aperture distribution is required? Evaluate the ratio

$$E_x(\lambda/(4 \sin \theta),0)/E_x(0, 0)$$

and sketch the complete aperture distribution.

3.4 Calculate the radiation pattern corresponding to the aperture distribution

$$E_x(x, 0) = \begin{cases} \cos^2(\pi x/a), & |x| < a/2 \\ 0, & |x| > a/2 \end{cases}$$

3.5 An approximate equivalent of a parabolic dish antenna is a square aperture with a half-cosine amplitude distribution in both principal directions. Deduce the gain of such an antenna in terms of its geometrical area and the wavelength. What is its aperture efficiency?

3.6 A square planar array with side a has an amplitude distribution which is the product of two triangular distributions in the directions parallel to the sides of the square, so that the amplitude is maximum at the centre and zero at the edges. The phase is constant over the array. Treating the antenna as a continuous aperture, calculate the radiation pattern. What is the level of the first sidelobe (in dB), relative to the main beam, in the two principal planes? Calculate the gain of the above aperture.

Chapter 4

4.1 A particular four element antenna array has element amplitudes 2, 1, -2, -1. Calculate the angular positions of the nulls in the radiation pattern when the inter-element spacing is (a) $\lambda/2$, (b) $\lambda/\sqrt{2}$, (c) $\lambda/(2\sqrt{2})$.

4.2 A four-element antenna array has element amplitudes 1, -1, 1, -1. Calculate the angular positions of the nulls in the radiation pattern when the inter-element spacing is (a) 0.5λ, (b) 0.2λ, (c) 0.8λ.

4.3 A four-element antenna array has an inter-element spacing $d = \lambda/(2\sqrt{2})$. It is required to produce a radiation pattern having nulls at $\theta = \pi/4$, $\pi/2$ and $3\pi/4$. Calculate the required element excitations.

4.4 A three-element array is to be used to produce a radiation pattern with nulls where $\cos\theta = \pm 1/(2\sqrt{3})$ and $\cos\theta = \pm\sqrt{(3)}/2$. Deduce the element spacing which allows you to do this, and the element excitations required.

Chapter 5

5.1 An anechoic chamber allows a distance of 5 metres between the antenna under test and the other antenna. Ignoring the size of the second antenna, estimate the limitations on size and frequency for antennas being tested. Give a graphical representation showing available combinations of size and frequency.

5.2 Two identical antennas are separated by 5 metres and are oriented for maximum power transfer. The power received by one is 20 dB down on that transmitted by the other, at a frequency of 6 GHz. Deduce the gain of the antennas (in dB). Was the use of a far field formula justified?

5.3 Derive (5.10) and (5.11) from (5.9).

Chapter 6

6.1 Derive the crossover levels quoted in figure 6.5.

Bibliography

Clarke, R. H. and Brown, J. (1980). *Diffraction Theory and Antennas*, Ellis Horwood, Chichester.

Collin, R. E. and Zucker, F. J. (1968). *Antenna Theory, Vols I and II*, McGraw-Hill, New York.

Elliott, R. S.(1981). *Antenna Theory and Design*, Prentice-Hall, Englewood Cliffs, New Jersey.

Hansen, R. C. (1964/1966). *Microwave Scanning Antennas, Vols I, II and III*, Academic Press, London.

Jasik, H. (1961). *Antenna Engineering Handbook*, McGraw-Hill, New York.

Jordan, E. C. and Balmain, K. G. (1968). *Electromagnetic Waves and Radiating Systems*, Prentice-Hall. Englewood Cliffs, New Jersey.

Kraus, J. D. (1950). *Antennas*, McGraw-Hill, New York.

Rudge, A. W., Milne, K., Olver, A. D. and Knight, P. (1982). *The Handbook of Antenna Design, Vols I and II*, Peter Peregrinus, Hitchin, Herts.

Silver, S. (1939). *Microwave Antenna Theory and Design*, McGraw-Hill, New York.

Steinberg, B. D. (1976). *Principles of Aperture and Array System Design*, Wiley, New York.

Stutzman, W. L. and Thiele, G. A. (1981). *Antenna Theory and Design*, Wiley, New York.

Answers to Exercises

2.3 $G = 1.5$ (1.76 dBi).

3.1 $P(\sin \alpha) = \dfrac{1}{2\pi} \left\{ \dfrac{ka}{1 - jka \sin \alpha} \right\}$.

3.3 $E_x(x, 0) = \dfrac{\pi \sin \theta_0 \cos(kx \sin \theta_0)}{(\pi/2)^2 - (kx \sin \theta_0)^2}$; ratio $= \pi/4$.

3.4 $P(S) = \dfrac{\sin(kaS/2)}{kaS/2} \cdot \dfrac{1}{1 - (kaS/2\pi)^2}$ (normalised form).

3.5 $G = \dfrac{4\pi A}{\lambda^2} \cdot \left(\dfrac{64}{\pi^4} \right)$.

3.6 $P(S_1, S_2) = E_0 \cdot \left(\dfrac{a}{2\lambda} \right)^2 \cdot \left\{ \dfrac{\sin(ka\, S_1/4)}{(ka\, S_1/4)} \right\}^2 \left\{ \dfrac{\sin(ka\, S_2/4)}{(ka\, S_2/4)} \right\}^2$;

   SLL $= -26$ dB; $G = \dfrac{4\pi a^2}{\lambda^2} \cdot \left(\dfrac{9}{16} \right)$.

4.1 (a) $\theta = 0,\ \ \pi/2,\ \pi$; (b) $\theta = \pi/4,\ \pi/2,\ 3\pi/4$; (c)$\theta = \pi/2$.
4.2 (a) $\theta = \pi/3,\ \pi/2,\ 2\pi/3$; (b) $\theta = \pi/2$;
   (c) $\theta = \pi/2$, $\cos \theta = \pm 5/16$, $\cos \theta = \pm 15/16$.
4.3 $1, -1, 1, -1$.
4.4 $d = (\sqrt{(3)}/2)\lambda$; $1, 0, 1$ (simplest answer).
5.1 $f > 0.6$, $d < 0.5$ and $d^2 f < 0.75$ (d in metres, f in GHz).
5.2 $G = 21.0$ dB. Yes, $2d^2/\lambda \approx 1$ m.

Index